TO ME, *Then* THROUGH

Learning the Unforced Rhythms of Grace

MARISA OWEN

UNITED HOUSE

To Me, Then Through Me—Copyright ©2020 by Marisa Owen
Published by UNITED HOUSE Publishing

Scriptures marked (ESV) are from The ESV® Bible (The Holy Bible, English Standard Version®), copyright © 2001 by Crossway, a publishing ministry of Good News Publishers. Used by permission. All rights reserved.

Scriptures marked (NIV) are from THE HOLY BIBLE, NEW INTERNATIONAL VERSION® NIV® Copyright © 1973, 1978, 1984 by International Bible Society® Used by permission. All rights reserved worldwide.

Scripture marked (KJV) are taken from The Authorized (King James) Version. Rights in the Authorized Version in the United Kingdom are vested in the Crown. Reproduced by permission of the Crown's patentee, Cambridge University Press

Scripture marked (NLT) are taken from the Holy Bible, New Living Translation, copyright © 1996, 2004, 2015 by Tyndale House Foundation. Used by permission of Tyndale House Publishers, Inc., Carol Stream, Illinois 60188. All rights reserved.

ISBN: 978-1-7327194-9-1

UNITED HOUSE Publishing
Waterford, Michigan
info@unitedhousepublishing.com
www.unitedhousepublishing.com

Cover and interior design: Matt Russell, Marketing Image, mrussell@marketing-image.com

Printed in the United States of America
2020—First Edition

SPECIAL SALES
Most UNITED HOUSE books are available at special quantity discounts when purchased in bulk by corporations, organizations, and special-interest groups. For information, please e-mail orders@ unitedhousepublishing.com.

Dedicated to my family, and to all who encouraged me to put these devotions into a collection. Thank you. I love y'all!

Table of Contents

Foreword 10

Introduction 12

A Spirit of Excellence 14

Change the Atmosphere! 16

Enjoy the Journey 18

Invading Territories and Carrying Out Assignments 20

Overflow With Confidence 22

Not of this World 24

Don't Skimp on the Helmet 26

A Piece of Your Mind or Peace of Mind? 28

Needs-Driven Kids 30

Never Be Enough 32

Drowning Out the Enemy's Voice 34

What Good is a Truck in the Driveway? 36

Improvise, Adapt, and Overcome 38

Funhouse Mirrors and Mazes 40

What are Seeds For? 42

Thoughts and Whispers 44

Sewer Water or Living Water? 46

Dancing in the Fire 48

The Danger of Comparison 50

Divine Connection to a Framing Nailer 52

Memorial Day Celebration 54

Unanswered Prayers 56

How to Be Angry and Sin Not 58

Free Indeed! 60

How Big is Our God? 62

Reminders of His Presence 64

One Decision, Many Victories 66

Let Truth Set You Free! 68

It is Well With My Soul 70

Be a Believing Believer 72

Far From Oppression 74

Are You Holding Peace While Holding Your Peace? 76

Wisdom, The Hearing Heart 78

You Need a Bath! 80

Dream Big! 82

You're a Good Tree! 84

The Greatest Miracle 88

For the Word's Sake 90

Where Y'all From? 92

Don't Go Back! 94

Encouraging Yourself in the Lord! 96

End the Debate 98

Then, All of a Sudden! 100

Dealing With Failed Expectations 102

Your Eyes Are in Front of Your Head 104

Releasing Forgiveness 106

New Wine in Old Wine Skins 108

Let the First Thing Be the First Thing 110

The Power of Grace 112

Captain America: Civil War 114

Sympathy vs. Compassion 116

Hurt Because of You or Hurting For You? 118

Loving Hell Out of People 120

God Doesn't Waste Anything 122

What or Who is Shepherding You? 124

What's that Smell? 126

Understanding Authority and Releasing Power! 128

Free From a Slave Mentality 130

Come Up Here! 132

Just One Door 134

Eating With Jesus 136

Love Doesn't Mean the Absence of Conflict 138

Contend for the Faith 140

Freedom From Manipulation 142

We Were Worth Leaving Heaven For 144

Got Peace? 146

Trying or Being? 148

The Word and His Voice 150

Storm Damage and Hope 152

Faith and Authority 154

Don't Partner with Fear 156

Hopeful New Year! 158

Hard Truth Wrapped in Love 160

Handling Heart Questions 162

How Much Do You Want to Spend? 164

What Did I Just Step Into?............................... 166

Servants, Sons, and Friends.............................. 168

Secondhand Lions 170

Letting God Judge Your Heart............................ 172

Just How Sure is Your Foundation?....................... 174

King of the Jungle 176

Why We Worship....................................... 180

Let Me Shed Some Light on that For You.................. 182

To Me, Then Through Me 184

Finding the Joy.. 186

Bride vs. Concubine 188

In Over Our Heads 190

Give Me Some of That!................................. 192

Check Your Heart 194

Vain Thought, Vain Talk 196

Living Memorials 198

A Bad Sensor.. 200

Unity 202

Time to Grow Up! 204

Distracted. 206

Don't Sit in the Ashes 208

What's Your Motivation?. 210

Compassion Without Compromise 212

Free from Guilt and Shame! 214

Defend, Debate, or Denounce? 216

Jesus Didn't Die Because I Was a Sinner 218

Are You Hangry?. 220

Fearing Man or Fearing God? 222

Intense Pruning 224

Don't Become What You're Going Through 226

Rescues Ain't Always Pretty 228

Heart vs. Law. 230

Don't Lose Your Grip!. 232

Renewing The Analytical Mind 234

The Right Tool for the Job. 236

Praying for a Loved One's Salvation 238

Living By Faith 242

Awaken the Passion 244

Acknowledgements 247

Notes 248

About the Author. 251

Foreword

If I were sharing the following words handwritten on paper with a pen, you would have to read between my tear splotches. These tears are akin to the ones shed as we absorb the melodies of a stirring symphony, drink in the beauty of the Grand Canyon, or witness an adoring couple exchanging wedding vows. Every aspect of author Marisa Owen's life is a pure extract of a beauty that Christ himself has distilled. We cry when we experience these moments because they are genuine and therefore deeply moving. Marisa and this devotional work expounding on grace are exactly that. According to Merriam Webster's dictionary, "genuine" means: "sincere; actually having the reputed qualities; actually produced by or proceeding from the alleged source or author; sincerely and honestly felt or experienced." I'm teary because I've already been a happy sojourner on the journey you're about to embark upon between the pages of this book. Each entry holds a rich treasury of wisdom proceeding from the Holy Spirit which Marisa tried and found true.

My husband, Al Brice (Marisa's Pastor) and I have shared your anticipation of reading the contents of *To Me, Then Through Me, Learning the Unforced Rhythms of Grace* over months and years. We loved Marisa's personal Facebook devotions so much, we requested that she share them with our church family each year during our Daniel Fast. Additionally, I asked her to post them routinely on our Women's Ministry Instagram account. We were delighted when she agreed to offer these open windows into her heart because we could attest to the impact of the wit and depth of her musings.

As soon as I personally read Marisa's devotions, I began urging her to publish them to a larger audience. I admitted there is no shortage of great devotionals these days, but *To Me, Then Through Me* is sure to become a beloved and acclaimed work because of her unique spin on age-old truths. Marisa skillfully captures the heartbeat of the Father toward His own. When I read other devotionals, I can pretty much predict the next paragraph on most topics because they tend to be rote. Not so with this author. Her words spring forth like wildflowers on well-worn paths. Though the passageways are ancient, her perspective evokes fresh insight. If you know Marisa, you aren't surprised that her words echo her unique persona.

And so, my tears are not only as a result of my happiness that you too will be enriched by these writings but even more so that you will begin to know a profoundly kind and genuine daughter of God. I know this because Marisa Owen has been a sister-friend and co-laborer in the kingdom for close to two decades. The essence of the Lover of Our Souls fills the room when she walks in. Her easy southern charm mingles with a sincere love for those for which her Savior died. With these words, I hasten to invite you into pages that will deeply touch your spirit and instruct your soul. I am certain that this will become a cherished work in your library that you will revisit—time and time again.

Tava Brice
Cofounder, Covenant Love Church
Fayetteville, NC

Introduction

For most of my Christian life, I genuinely tried to fit the mold of what I *thought* God wanted me to *do*. I did all the Christian things: worshiped, begged in prayer, and willed myself to *be more* than I saw in the mirror. Tired of feeling like a hypocrite, I went my own way for a while. Even then, God had a vexing sense of humor. In college, I tried to hide from God but would find myself unwittingly ministering to the lost. I could almost hear God chuckle as I fumed at Him for interrupting my good time! Slowly, patiently, and lovingly, He kept tugging at my heart, wooing me back. Post-college, I married a great Christian man, ministered in a Christian rock band, and tried to be the perfect mom. I was attempting to live the Christian life while continuing to drag my insecurities and failures behind me. It was exhausting!

It was only when I began to submit my thoughts and emotions to His love that I understood how much He wanted to be with me and for me to just *be His kid*! Me… of all people! But, if you read Isaiah 61, you'll see He's actually drawn to the humble, afflicted, and brokenhearted. He was sent to heal the wounds of the brokenhearted, to tell captives, "You are free," and to tell prisoners, "Be free from your darkness" (MSG, my paraphrase). We are the very ones He calls to restore the wastelands, ruined cities, and desolations of past generations.

These personal devotions were written as He taught me to filter life through grace and love; first towards me, then through me. I have determined to hold my thoughts and feelings accountable to God's Word. Holy Spirit is the teacher, while Jesus is the measuring stick. I'm willing to be *comfortably uncomfortable* with what I don't yet see; for me, *that* is faith.

No words sum up the relationship He wants with you and me more than Matthew 11:28-30 (MSG, emphasis added) where Jesus says, "Are you tired? Worn out? Burned out on religion? Come to me. Get away with me and you'll recover your life. I'll show you how to take a *real* rest. Walk with me and work with me—watch how I do it. *Learn the unforced rhythms of grace.* I won't lay anything heavy or ill-fitting on you. Keep company with me and you'll learn to live freely and lightly."

As you read and digest these pages, I pray that God will give you peace beyond your understanding and love without measure! May God glory in your testimony as you become a roadmap for others. Get so close to Jesus, you can no longer distinguish between His heartbeat and your own! Allow Holy Spirit to transform the very way you think, refining your natural discernment through His heart of compassion. His heart never wears out, and His love never fails!

So, grab your notebooks! Be sure to read the scriptures referenced in each one, and write what God is revealing to you. Let it become a part of you, flowing through you—in unforced rhythms of His grace!

Peace, y'all!

Marisa

A Spirit of Excellence

READ

Romans 12:11-13,

Daniel 2:46,

Daniel 6:16-28,

Matthew 5:7-16,

Proverbs 4:18-19,

James 1

Daniel is one of the most amazing young men in the Bible! He faithfully served God under several different leaders. When his country was conquered, he was taken from his family as a young man, chosen for his looks and intelligence. He was castrated (possibly), indoctrinated, reeducated, and forced to serve unrighteous kings. At one point, he was marginalized as just another fortune teller by those who didn't know his God. God had given him the ability to interpret signs and translate dreams.

Throughout his account, Daniel always keeps his heart from becoming offended. Daniel never bowed to pressure from men. He didn't accept the flavor-of-the-day culture. He wouldn't turn from his God. How did he stay so unaffected by it all? How is it he served with such goodness and wisdom despite such conditions? He was even loved by a king who was tricked into throwing Daniel into the lion's den. The king worried all night until he could run to the den to check on him the next morning!

God granted Daniel favor, even when he was being lied about, so that kings, even evil ones, would come to respect and trust Daniel for his spirit of excellence! Somehow, no matter the injustice he endured, his passion for his God kept his heart free from his right to maintain anger and bitterness. It wasn't that he was out trying to make people straighten up but simply living his life unto God, serving with a spirit of excellence, manifesting Godly wisdom, humility, and love in every action. As a result, his life impacted a nation.

As Christians, we are called to that same excellence of spirit. We can't change our past, but we can change how we see it. We can't keep everyone around us from being offended, but we can keep ourselves from offense and live above the lies, misconceptions, and whispers. What we must do is love the unlovable and serve God with excellence.

We are called to be light, and light is needed in dark places. It does not do the world any good to keep all of our light inside the four walls of the church while everyone else wanders in the darkness outside. Light doesn't have to force its way into dark places. It doesn't beat darkness over the head. It just shines! To those who are accustomed to the dark, and prefer it, it only hurts their eyes, and they'll turn away. But others looking for a light by which to see will be attracted by the light and warmth of our fire.

Let's be careful to not lose sight of God when we're in trials. Let's not be known for offense, strife, and division. Let's determine to have a heart submitted to God, free from the effects of persecution and injustice so others will see us and glorify our Father.

GRAB YOUR JOURNAL!

What is God showing you at this moment?

In light of this revelation, how does this shift your thoughts and actions?

Change the Atmosphere!

READ

Matthew 10:11-13,

Luke 10:5-9,

Philippians 4:6-9,

Romans 14:17-19,

Philippians 2:1-5 & 12-17,

Jude 1:20-23

Have you ever noticed how one person's attitude can affect an entire group of people? The angry relative who brings drama to the family reunion, or when the boss walks in with a serious look on his face that sends dread through the office, or the enthusiastic leader who can rally the troops. Teachers can tell you how *one* student can affect an entire class. Even our dogs can sense our moods! We actually release the attitudes that overshadow us.

During Vacation Bible School one year, I talked about how God made us to be like salt. I explained that salt preserves; it draws flavor from whatever food it's added to, and it also does something else. I showed the children an experiment. I took a raw egg and carefully placed it into a glass of water, where it sank to the bottom. Pulling it out again, I slowly added quite a bit of salt to the water and had a student stir. Upon putting the egg back in the water, we noticed how the salt had changed the density of the water, and the egg floated.

Just as salt changed the atmospheric condition of the water, we have been positioned to change the atmosphere wherever we are sprinkled into society. When we're squeezed by the pressures of life, what is in us will be revealed, and our attitudes will inevitably ooze out in our actions. We can't release what hasn't been developed in us, so we need to build ourselves up in the holiest faith (Jude 1:20).

Jesus told the disciples to release peace to the households which received them (Luke 10:5-6 NIV). Peace, righteousness, and joy in the Holy Ghost are all results of our citizenship in the Kingdom of God. When we receive the revelation of our Kingdom identity and live our lives as citizens of Heaven, we will draw from those rich stores. It will be what comes out of us when the atmosphere is less than favorable. Then, instead of being *affected* by attitudes and circumstances, we will be the catalyst effecting change for those around us.

We can bring a calming word in the midst of chaos. We can smile in the long line at Walmart when the cashier is slow because we're not "waiting"—we're on assignment! If we get stuck in traffic, instead of wasting it, complaining and angry, we can redeem the time, ministering to God! (It's not like our attitude can make them go faster, so why not let Holy Spirit make an adjustment in us?) Instead of empowering negative attitudes in others by agreeing with them, *we can allow the mind of Christ to take over!* Let's be salt and light and *change* the atmosphere wherever we go!

GRAB YOUR JOURNAL!

What is God showing you at this moment?

In light of this revelation, how does this shift your thoughts and actions?

Enjoy the Journey

READ

Luke 7:18-23,

2 Corinthians 12:7-10,

Matthew 6:33,

1 Kings 19:11-13,

Romans 1:17,

James 1:2-8,

James 1:12-13,

James 1:22-25,

1 John 2:20-21,

Romans 14:19,

Hebrews 12:14

One of our favorite things to do at Christmas was to give our kids gifts that were too big to wrap. Instead of wrapping, we would send them on a scavenger hunt. We'd start off with a small gift box containing a note, which would lead them to another hint, then another until they found their gift. Not one time did they sit back and pout about the journey. Every clue was filled with giggles and anticipation.

Often, when we're learning to hear God's voice for a specific calling or direction, we're looking for the present to be neatly wrapped and presented. We want Moses' burning bush experience so there will be absolutely *no way* we can mess up! We want a flashing neon sign pointing the way so we know it's God. *But, where's the faith in that?* How does that *build relationship?*

God may give us the end result without revealing how He plans to get us there, as He did with Joseph, the dreamer. Or, He may give us step one. Depending on the size of the call, many of us would buckle under the weight of what might be expected of us. So, He leads us from faith to faith, never throwing us into a battle He doesn't equip us to win. He never leads us into a situation He will not empower us to go through. When Paul asked God to remove the messenger of Satan sent to buffet him, God replied, "... My grace is sufficient for you, for My strength is made perfect in weakness" (2 Corinthians 12:9 NKJV). When John the Baptist was sentenced to death and sent word to ask Jesus if He was really the Messiah, Jesus replied, "Tell John all that's going on, and blessed are those who are not offended in Me" (Luke 7:23, my paraphrase).

Romans 1:17 (AMP) says it this way, "For in the gospel the righteousness of

God is revealed, *both springing from* faith *and leading to* faith [disclosed in a way that awakens more faith]."

We are on a *journey* of faith, which means we are in a constant mode of "mystery to be revealed." It is when we step out of faith, we become weary of the journey, asking, "Why?" (Which, most of the time, if we're honest, is insinuating to God we just don't approve of His parenting style). The answer is in there somewhere, but He is building something in us along the way which requires us to trust in Him.

Let's not look simply for the immediate, but rather embrace every step, knowing we're not alone, listening for and leaning into the still small voice, the anointing from Holy Spirit on our scavenger hunt with Him!

GRAB YOUR JOURNAL!

What is God showing you at this moment?

In light of this revelation, how does this shift your thoughts and actions?

Invading Territories and Carrying Out Assignments

READ

1 Chronicles 4:9-10,

2 Peter 2:5,

Matthew 5:16,

1 Peter 3:15,

1 Peter 2:4-10,

Acts 4:13-31,

Philippians 2:1-18

It doesn't take long to look at a territory and see who's in charge. We can tell if crime has taken over by the attitude on the street. We can guess the prosperity of a city by looking to see what the state government is doing to attract opportunity. We can tell when our place of employment is managed well or not. We can even look at the prosperity of our own soul and know if we are on the throne of our own heart or if God is ruling there.

In prayer the other day, I had a conviction come to me: "How's your territory?" As I thought more about it, I remembered Jabez's prayer in 1 Chronicles 4:10 (AMPC), "... Oh, that You would bless me and enlarge my border, and that Your hand might be with me, and You would keep me from evil so it might not hurt me!"

Our territories are our jobs, communities, and families, and we have assignments on our journey through life. Sometimes our assignments might require us walking through fire, or sleeping in a lion's den to change the spiritual authority of our territory, but our primary purpose is to represent Christ. We kneel before God as priests, then through our obedience, we, as kings, serve notice to the spiritual rulers of darkness, take back ground which was lost, and then, God is glorified.

As representatives of God's kingdom, what is our border? It's our sphere of influence for His glory. In other words, how is my life affecting those around me? My co-workers? My children? My neighborhood?

People watch our lives. They watch how we navigate trials. They watch how we deal with pain. Some may watch and never change, but they should never be able to dismiss us because of our submission to the authority of Christ. Our greatest testimony is our continuance in faith, never wavering in any circumstance.

I want to emphasize, though, that while we influence those around us, we do not have control over them; their condition may not always reflect our preference. Before we go into self-condemnation, we have to remember that Noah never had a convert in 100 years, and even God's first two children failed in a near-perfect environment.

Let's go before God as priests to His throne and see how to best influence our territories as kings on assignment. Let's seek His will and purpose and watch Him bring Heaven to Earth through us!

GRAB YOUR JOURNAL!

What is God showing you at this moment?

In light of this revelation, how does this shift your thoughts and actions?

Overflow With Confidence

READ

John 10:24-29,

2 Corinthians 4,

James 4:7,

2 Corinthians 10:3-7,

Jeremiah 29:11-13,

Romans 5:25,

Romans 15:13,

Hebrews 11:1,

2 Timothy 1:7,

1 John 3:19-23

Growing up, I wasn't one of the "pretty" girls. I wasn't popular. I was neither stylish nor thin. I was "okay" at a lot of things but never the best at anything. I tended to put myself down a lot and was desperate for anyone to validate my existence. As I got older, I developed a strong, outgoing personality to mask my insecurities. It was exhausting to keep up the illusion that I was a confident, fulfilled young woman and mom.

Even though I grew up in church and had knowledge of God's Word, I still had not died to self in acceptance through performance. Low self-esteem remained a filter for everything I did and fought against everything I longed to be. That insecure voice in the back of my mind kept trying to live up to an impossible standard that I had created.

One day after a women's meeting at our new church, our pastor's wife, Tava Brice, who didn't know me at all at that time, had a word of knowledge from Holy Spirit for me. While praying, she had a mental picture of me walking, but it seemed everywhere I went, there was a pack of dogs nipping at my heels. Tava didn't fully know what it meant, but I did. Those demanding dogs bullied me to try and fit some impossible standard to be accepted. I don't remember everything she said, but that was the first time I felt like God *saw* me. Tava's words to me were the starting point which allowed God to bring the revelation of His love, bringing peace to a weary soul.

When we come to Christ, we will never see ourselves the way He does, until we are willing to die to our vision of self. Speaker and senior pastor Bill at Bethel Church in California said: "I can't afford to have thoughts in my head about me that God doesn't have in His."[1] At the very least, false identity stifles our gifts.

At most, it drives us to try to earn or attain what God has already given. His Name, His identity, His authority, His love, His acceptance, and His forgiveness are all ours!

There are many voices crying out in our mind, "I'm not ready", "I'm not good enough", "I might disappoint", "They don't approve of me!" Then, there is the still small voice we must give place to. The heart's cry which hopes against hope and believes in the face of all doubt. Our Father's voice, calling, "Get up! Don't quit! I am with you. Stand." We must learn to hone in on our Father's voice (John 10:4-5).

His voice called a scared rabbit of a man named Gideon "mighty man of valor" (Judges 6:12 NKJV). His voice called a shepherd boy "King" (1 Samuel 16:1). His voice made Moses, the stutterer, His mouthpiece (Exodus 4:10). His voice made water a path to walk on (Matthew 14:25).

It is His voice which resonates into the areas of our lives that seem impossible to master and causes them to bow! It is His voice that calls light to come out of darkness (2 Corinthians 4:6).

Let's stop entertaining those deceptive "self" filled thoughts that have been the center of our universe, which we've allowed to sit on the throne of our hearts. Let's chase off those dogs who keep nipping at us as we take authority over them and submit ourselves to God's thoughts toward us.

Romans 15:13 (AMP): "May the God of hope fill you with all joy and peace in believing [through the experience of your faith] that by the power of the Holy Spirit you will abound in hope and overflow with confidence in His promises."

We are loved. We are wanted. We are accepted! Now build on that!

GRAB YOUR JOURNAL!

What is God showing you at this moment?

In light of this revelation, how does this shift your thoughts and actions?

Not of this World

READ

2 Timothy 3:1-7,

Isaiah 26:3,

Colossians 3:1-17

I was reading the story of Christian martyr Polycarp, probably the pastor of the Smyrna church mentioned in Revelations 2, who lived during the most dangerous time in Christian history. It is believed he may have been discipled by the Apostle John. God had shown him in a dream what was to happen to him, yet he chose not to run when the soldiers came to arrest him. Instead, he offered them food and rest, then asked if he might first pray for an hour. They saw no harm in granting his request, and he prayed with such tenderness and fervor they apologized for having to carry out their command. When Caesar threatened him with death, he simply replied, "Eighty-six years I have been his servant. How can I blaspheme my King who saved me?"[2]

As they prepared Polycarp for burning at the stake, they planned to nail him to it to keep him still during the process, but he informed them it wouldn't be necessary because God would give him the grace to endure. As the fire raged, it curled away from Polycarp, and he stood untouched, simply glowing. The executioner was finally ordered to end him by dagger and his blood extinguished the flames. The crowd witnessed a miracle.

Many of the accounts in *Foxe's Book of Martyrs* mentions the way Christians seemed to have a peace about them; so much so, in fact, it appeared to those who witnessed their executions, they were either not in their body or Jesus was talking to them as they endured. The miraculous death of Polycarp brought an end to the persecution of the church.[3]

Most of us can't fully understand the sacrifice paid by the early church during the years of persecution. We may not suffer the same societal pressures or internal battle that correspond. But, we can understand having to make the choice between following after form or diving into a relationship. When we reduce the gospel to a prayer to be prayed, a lifestyle of religion, focusing only on our own blessings, instead of becoming a blessing, we exclude the power of Christ seen so evidently in the early martyrs (2 Timothy 3:5).

Too often, we succumb to emotional responses because of hardships which arise from living in a fallen world, rather than responding as if we were *actually* the physical body of Christ. We may feel as though we are hypocrites if we choose to worship when we feel guilty, tired, or frustrated because we don't want to give God an unworthy offering. At times we think we should try to hide in our sin, much like Adam, when the door to His throne is for mercy and grace. There is power in worship when it is sacrificial.

To worship when things are going well is a celebration, but worshiping when life is beating us down invites the power of God to keep us calm and courageous through the fire. Fire may burn up weeds, but it purifies gold. So, the fire of persecution burns and purifies our faith. Light doesn't stand out until it is in a dark place. Peace becomes evident when all hell is breaking loose around us, and we remain unmoved by the trial. I love this quote by Bill Johnson, "You only have authority over the storm you can sleep in."[4]

Let's experience peace in the storm as we worship during the toughest of trials. Let's be so deep in relationship with Holy Spirit that the fire He places inside us diminishes the strength of the fire around us.

GRAB YOUR JOURNAL!

What is God showing you at this moment?

In light of this revelation, how does this shift your thoughts and actions?

Don't Skimp on the Helmet

READ

Ephesians 6:10-18,

Hosea 4:6,

2 Corinthians 10:2-5,

Romans 10:3-4,

Romans 10:15,

Romans 12:1-2,

John 8:32,

2 Corinthians 2:11,

John 14:20-22

Dirt bikes were part of our children's lives from the age of four until sixteen when they could drive a car. Of course, we made sure they looked like stormtroopers from *Star Wars*, with chest protectors, boots, gloves, and helmets. When picking out the helmet, our kids wanted the coolest looking one, but our job was to choose the safest one. There are a few different qualities of helmets, but a parent doesn't skimp on the part which needs the most protection. It must meet the highest crash rating standards because a young rider *will* eventually crash, and their degree of protection determines how quickly they recover from the fall.

Ephesians 6 tells us to put on the full armor of God, and *above all*, lift up the shield of faith, take the helmet of salvation, and the sword of the Spirit. Salvation is not just "our eventual trip to Heaven." Our renewed mind is included in our salvation, which brings peace, healing, deliverance, protection, safety, and redemption. When we are born again, our spirit comes alive and is made perfect, but our soul (mind, will, and emotions) needs to be renewed in everything this new life encompasses, which results in strength and protection (Hosea 4:6).

How often do we become offended, hurt, disappointed, or burned-out over failed expectations for God and life? Is it simply because we lack understanding of salvation? Self-preserving thoughts and human reasoning come through our five senses and past experiences, and many times, they fight against what God says is truth. The Devil hands us bricks of hurt and offense, and frequently we cement them with words that flow from a struggling heart, building walls which become prisons, which can keep us from our destiny and identity. We tear these walls down and drive out the enemy by agreeing in obedience. This is when our helmet is doing what it is designed to do! The helmet of salvation is designed not only to protect our minds from attacks of our enemy, but to protect our born-again identity as children of God. It encapsulates our minds so we won't be torn away by lies.

We become competent warriors, wielding our Sword (God's Word) and the shield of faith, when we understand who we are in Christ. Walking out our mission, knowing the plan of the enemy, we are better prepared to defend ourselves against everything that would exalt itself against the knowledge of Christ (2 Corinthians 10:5)!

Let's get into His presence and allow Him to reveal and fortify our hearts and minds to total salvation; not just living for the hereafter, but so we don't compromise the life we were recreated and reborn for. Let's go after God with total abandonment, knowing the better life He has for us.

What lies have we built to protect ourselves against the Truth of *who God says we are?*

Let His helmet of salvation do what it does—save, make well, restore, preserve, and recover. Then, we'll crush the Devil's influence everywhere we go with the gospel of Christ!

GRAB YOUR JOURNAL!

What is God showing you at this moment?

In light of this revelation, how does this shift your thoughts and actions?

A Piece of Your Mind or Peace of Mind?

READ
Psalms 23,
Romans 10:17,
Colossians 2:2-15,
Galatians 5:1,13-25,
Galatians 2:10,
Hebrews 5:7-14,
Matthew 6:22-23,
Matthew 13:11-14,
Matthew 10:38,
Mark 8:34;
Luke 9:23;
Luke 14:27

I really struggled with anger for a large part of my life. It was more of an inward issue stemming from the frustration of low self-esteem, revealing itself more upon becoming a parent. All of the door-slamming, heavy foot-walking, passive-aggressive comments, and guilt-bomb launches to bring those I loved most into alignment were powerful manipulative tools in my passive-aggressive arsenal.

I was a Christian, yet I was acting in *total selfishness*. I grew up in a church which really taught God's Word, with parents who tried hard to live it. So, it wasn't that I didn't want to love; it was that I didn't know *how* to walk in love. I had accepted Christ, but I can picture Him trying to find a place to sit amongst the chaos in my heart. He seemed to be on reserve for cleaning up the messes I made.

It wasn't until I got tired of losing my temper and making others miserable, I purposed to change. I knew the fruits of the Spirit were love, joy, peace, patience, kindness, goodness, faithfulness, gentleness, and self-control (Galatians 5:22-23a), but I didn't know how to cultivate them. At first, I tried to "control" anger, biting my tongue and struggling against the desire to lash out (and there is *definitely* a place for obedience in this area).

But, God desires our surrender to His changing power so obedience isn't a dire struggle but rather a journey with a friend through tough times. Romans 12:2 says to *renew* our minds and to not be conformed to the world. Why? Being born again may get us to Heaven, but renewing our mind gets Heaven into us. When dying to self becomes more important than my attempt to maintain control over others, I will begin to see God's perspective.

Our hearts begin to shift as we start understanding love as the essence of God, and our lives are not about us but rather our purpose and who we are is for Christ and in Christ. The more we renew our minds and submit to His will, the more freely Holy Spirit is able to move in us. When we strive to make ourselves receptive to Him and deny self, He begins to redirect our attitudes and actions. It doesn't happen overnight, and there will forever be the decision to continually humble ourselves under His hand. With every failure, there is an opportunity to dig in so we can grow. With every success, there is an opportunity to prune pride and self-righteousness.

It's the implanted Word taking shape inside which changes us from the inside out. Not just the Word we read and quote, but the Word we digest in God's presence (Psalms 23:5). Faith comes by *hearing* (Romans 10:17), not having *heard*. Hearing is present tense. Hearing is what God is saying and revealing to us through His Word at the moment. As God's revelation flows into us, it expands our capacity to receive even more. The more we receive, the greater the increase (Matthew 13:12). Then, we are to use it to influence the world around us.

Let us direct our vision on one thing and focus on the love of Christ toward us and through us, practicing what we have heard, sharpening our spiritual senses (Hebrews 5:14). Let's allow Holy Spirit to bring us into supernatural *peace* so we can *pour out the peace* of our mind instead of giving someone *a piece* of our mind.

GRAB YOUR JOURNAL! | *What is God showing you at this moment?*

In light of this revelation, how does this shift your thoughts and actions?

Needs-Driven Kids

READ

Genesis 2:18 (AMP),

Ephesians 5:1-14,

Philippians 2:1-18,

Romans 13:8

You can gain a lot of insight into kids' lives when they are in a classroom. Put twenty of those little ones in a room, and you can see the timid one, the class clown, the self-confidence of one who knows they are loved by a parent, and the ones who yearn for attention they don't get at home for one reason or another. Sadly, no matter how much our society tries to legislate a level playing field, what's in the heart will manifest in their actions.

One particular little first grade girl I taught was so hungry for love and acceptance, she would do most anything for it. She rarely had her homework, never returned signed paperwork, and a parent had not ever attended scheduled meetings. She rushed through her work to show me she was the first one to finish. If she was reprimanded for a negative behavior, she instantly tried to do something she thought praiseworthy and told us immediately, fishing for reaffirmation.

It was difficult not to instantly reaffirm her effort to make up for her transgression. After all, the child was obviously needy in this area. But, a good teacher doesn't just want behavior modification, as it only teaches them to manipulate others. They want to ignite a desire for excellence which will take them out of chaos, abuse, or neglect, and *allow them to choose* something better for their future.

Those without Christ tend to live like this because they are apart from love. A neediness has crept into the large majority of the church. We are *so in need* of love because we haven't learned to *become* love.

We believe people, even our spouses, are there to fill a need because we desire affirmation and acceptance. Instead of allowing God's perfect love to flow through us to our marriages and relationships, we look for them to manifest it themselves! God didn't give Adam a wife because he was lonely. He was alone but fulfilled. God gave him Eve so the *two* could become a stronger *one*. Our prayer should be for the revelation that we are fully loved and accepted in Christ; that we may love others rather than need to be loved by others.

Man was created in the likeness of God, so he was without "need." Need only came after the fall of man when he became separated from love. The need for love was birthed in all of us, and our desperation for it often drives us to give up who we are in the process. Jesus died to restore our identity. If we submit to anyone or anything less, we'll always be lacking in some way. If we identify with Christ, dying to self, we will be less likely to fall into the trap of trying to please and be accepted by others. The Devil has had a few thousand years' practice at deception and has made us believe we have to manipulate our way into love and acceptance.

The only way we'll truly find love is through the revelation of our identity as one who is *already* beloved in Christ. We are conformed into the image of Jesus and learn to die to our selfish ways as we understand we are accepted and loved by God.

Let's not allow ourselves to get trapped into performing or manipulating at the expense of others, but owing no one anything but to love, without expectation of return! Let's meditate on how much we are loved and accepted by our Father.

GRAB YOUR JOURNAL! | *What is God showing you at this moment?*
| *In light of this revelation, how does this shift your thoughts and actions?*

Never Enough

READ

John 4:7-35,

John 5:37-47,

Haggai 1:6-7,

Romans 12:1-2,

John 11:25-26,

Luke 9:57-62,

Jeremiah 17:5-8,

Ephesians 1:4-7,

Luke 10:16

The movie *The Greatest Showman* is so worth watching! It is a fictional account of P.T. Barnum's circus. My husband reluctantly bought it, thinking it would be a "one and done," but, to give you an idea of how many times we've watched it, we've memorized the songs. It's the story of a poor boy trying to make it big. He gathers a cast of misfits who have lived hidden away, bringing them together to find family and acceptance. Barnum nearly loses everything before he realizes the success he thirsted for was only a vapor.

In my opinion, both the movie and its music are masterpieces, and one hauntingly powerful song is called "Never Enough." It describes Barnum's constant thirst for success, his need to prove his worth. A thousand spotlights and golden towers weren't enough because he still self-identified as a pauper. His glory always faded with each close of a curtain, and the thirst for more drove him to the brink of losing his family.

In John 4, Jesus met the Samaritan woman at the well. Not only were Samaritans considered outcasts by the Jews, but she personally had other reasons to live in shame. This woman had been married and divorced four times, and when Jesus met her, she was living with a man she was not married to.. She had probably come to the well later in the day, after the other women had drawn, to avoid the tongue-waggers. More than likely, she dealt with low self-esteem from either commitment issues, shame, or having been rejected so many times. There was obviously a void in her soul, a thirst. Jesus offered her living water that will never run dry.

Many of us come into church trying to fill a void, searching for a sense of belonging, hoping a new pool of potential friends will make us feel good about ourselves. We strive for God's approval by being good, moral people with Christian as our title. After all, fitting in should be effortless where people are commanded to love. But, if we only bring our emptiness and huge expectations for others to fill instead of looking to transform ourselves we'll become disheartened and detached from church or from God altogether. While I am all about church family, it's unfair to expect people to fill that void.

We're not supposed to be pouring water into empty wells. We dig deep until we hit water! We can't fill from the outside what can only be filled if it's springing up from the inside. There is nothing in the world, the church, or service we perform, that will satisfy the desire for purpose, significance, destiny, and belonging. Whatever we gain through striving, we will struggle to maintain. It will *never be enough.*

Jesus desires to be our source of life. He wants to *possess us fully* in our attitudes, desires, victories, and our broken parts, so when people see us, they will see Him flowing from us. Our life will be a powerful wellspring of His life-giving love.

Only when we *receive the revelation* we are already accepted in Christ will we be impervious to rejection of man. We don't need a spotlight, social acceptance and approval, or a picture-perfect life. If we know Christ Jesus has made us *enough* before God, we won't continue striving to do it ourselves. We were made to find our identity and affirmation in Him.

GRAB YOUR JOURNAL! | *What is God showing you at this moment?*

In light of this revelation, how does this shift your thoughts and actions?

Drowning Out the Enemy's Voice

READ

John 10:1-5,

Lamentations 3:22-23,

1 Peter 5:7-11,

Romans 8:1,

James 5:7-10

Have you ever had one of those weeks where your focus has been on everything but God? Work, kids, obligations, exhaustion, and a wandering mind made you feel like you were far from the very One you needed to successfully navigate all of those things in the first place. The next thing you know, the Devil sticks his foot in the door of your mind and whispers how unworthy and selfish you are to go to God, after you've put Him last every day this week!

Last week was one of those weeks for me. Thoughts about staying home from church on Sunday to catch up on stuff came into my mind as I heard those little whispers. But, I've learned a thing or two about my Daddy's love for me and a lot about how the Devil works, so I didn't get caught in the trap of allowing guilt to keep me from running to God's arms and praising Him that His mercies are *new every morning!* So even though the Enemy's whispers didn't stop, I never acknowledged his voice.

When praise and worship started, I sang and clapped and danced. Then, the Enemy whispered, "Hypocrite." I began to thank God for His mercy, love, acceptance, and blessing.

Again I heard accusation, "You think God wants your leftovers? Do you think He really enjoys this display after the week you've given Him?" Like arrows to my heart, it was almost too much for me. So, I thanked God louder and danced a little harder, out of sheer rebellion against Satan.

Then God did something amazing which shut the Devil's mouth for the rest of the service. The roving camera person on stage focused his camera on the saxophone player for just a moment, and I heard God say, *"Look."* As big as day, I see my son. Instantly, I was undone! My husband and I prayed for quite a while for our son to come to Christ, and there he was, glorifying God with his music! Like a flood, the love of God came and drowned out every condemnation. Wrapped in a blanket of love, I was shielded from every fiery dart. Hopefully, my celebration didn't offend anyone because joy overtook my warring! The battle was over!

I know there will be times where my attention is drawn away. But, I won't make a habit of it because *I know* He loves me!

Remember, there is *no condemnation* for those in Christ! Pappa knows how to get our attention and keeps drawing us back so our minds are centered on Him! Let's not lose heart! We are not immune to hearing the Enemy's voice, but we don't have to *bow* to it. James 4:7 tells us to *submit to God*. In that very act, the Devil *is resisted*, and he's *got* to flee!

GRAB YOUR JOURNAL!

What is God showing you at this moment?

In light of this revelation, how does this shift your thoughts and actions?

What Good is a Truck in the Driveway?

READ

Acts 1:4-8,

Luke 10:9,

Luke 17:20-21,

Romans 12:1-2,

Matthew 5:14-16,

Romans 1:11-12,

John 17:1-26,

2 Timothy 3:15-17

What good would a brand new truck be if it only sat in your driveway? You could go out and admire it, wash it, sit in it, listen to the stereo, or even allow the neighbors to drive by and admire what you have, but until you use it, it's no good to you. Trucks have amazing power, designed for work, and meant to be used for more than just a passenger vehicle. They're made to haul things. Power is not profitable unless it is activated.

We need the infilling of Holy Spirit to navigate this life successfully. Why else would He tell those in the upper room not to leave until He came (See Acts 1:4)? But, the power of Holy Spirit in our lives is meant, not simply to enable us to live in this world, but to be carriers of the Kingdom of Heaven (Luke 10:9) and diffusers of Holy Spirit.

His power is available to us, but in order to walk in the fullness of it, we are required to lay down our very lives as a *living sacrifice* (Romans 12:1), which means giving up our right to maintain *man's* way of thinking and renewing ourselves to God's way of thinking. It means His passion becomes our passion. It means not entangling ourselves in this world to the point we are under the *influence* of political or religious systems (Mark 8:15).

Romans 12:2 tells us to be transformed and progressively changed into the image of Christ who is personified love. People who are not born again are incapable of anointed thought, so we are to be a *light* for them (Matthew 5:14), representing Jesus. When we are born again, we are continually transforming, so we need to encourage one another in the faith (Romans 1:12) rather than enable each other to stay offended, angry, depressed, or anxious. It's time to turn on the truck and get to work, encouraging those around us to do the same.

Good drivers know the rules of the road, know their vehicle, and know what they are going to use it for. Likewise, let's be humble and obedient students of God's Word, intimately becoming *one* with Christ (John 17:21), with teachable spirits. Let's be sensitive to His conviction, open to correction, quick to restoration, and trained in righteousness, so we may be "... complete *and* proficient, outfitted *and* thoroughly equipped for every good work" (2 Timothy 3:17 AMP).

GRAB YOUR JOURNAL!

What is God showing you at this moment?

In light of this revelation, how does this shift your thoughts and actions?

Improvise, Adapt, and Overcome

READ

2 Timothy 3,

Matthew 6:5-13,

Psalms 103:7,

Acts 17:28,

John 8:36,

1 John 2:20-21,

James 1:4

Currently, one of my new favorite TV shows is *SEAL Team*. I hope the story doesn't get hijacked by socio-political issues that will turn me off. I love that these soldiers are ready at a moments notice. They have a plan in place for every mission, knowing it could change and being prepared for every contingency. They rely on their comms (communication devices) for minute-to-minute intel from those who can see what they can't. They know the mechanics for reconnaissance, but their response depends on whatever is behind the door. They are elite warriors, citizens of a sovereign nation, and despite hardship or loss, their identity and purpose never change.

We are citizens of Heaven, tasked with evangelizing all of humanity. Our mission doesn't change, but how we go about it depends on intel from our Commander. He sees the hidden things behind the doors of people's hearts and snares laid by the Enemy. We may know the mechanics of evangelizing, but success depends on communication with Holy Spirit. We may see how sin surfaces out, but God wants to get to the roots hidden in the heart.

If we inadvertently make God into a formula, we'll become set in our ways and make our relationship with Holy Spirit a powerless, religious act. We cut our comms and then wonder why God suddenly seems unfaithful. But if God routinely answers prayers based on self-serving motives, it would only further our becoming more self-reliant and self-seeking (2 Timothy 3:5-7).

We want cookie-cutter solutions, patch jobs, or relief. But, God wants us to also have the inner peace which anchors us as we go through storms, so when we come out on the other side, our faith is stronger, more mature, and spiritual fruit is evident.

We are to live, function, and have our identity in Him (Acts 17:28 TPT). If *He sets us free*, we're *completely* free (John 8:36). If we *escape*, we tend to leave pieces behind. After all, are we indeed free from an enemy if we remain captive to unforgiveness or bitterness? We need a listening ear, a humble heart, and a renewed mind to remain free while we're still in the storm.

God has endless ways to get us where we need to be exactly when we need to be there; Whether we speak to the mountains or traverse them, fight like a warrior or wait expectantly like a child, we must listen, learn to submit, and stay sensitive to His leading. God's Word never changes.

So, by all means, let's discipline ourselves in study and prayer, but trust God with the unexpected, listening and discerning the prompting of Holy Spirit, to effectively fulfill our mission! Hooyah!

GRAB YOUR JOURNAL! | *What is God showing you at this moment?*

In light of this revelation, how does this shift your thoughts and actions?

Funhouse Mirrors and Mazes

READ

2 Corinthians 5:17,

2 Corinthians 10:3-7,

Romans 8:1-17,

James 1:19-26,

Genesis 1:27,

1 John 4:13-18,

John 3:16-17

If you've ever been through a funhouse maze of mirrors at a carnival, you've seen distorted images of yourself. Although they're fun to look at, you know that's not what you look like. The mirrors have been contorted to produce certain shapes and designs. Though you may be able to tell you are looking at yourself, it is not a true reflection. It is merely a labyrinth of pathways meant to keep you off-balance as you feel your way to an exit.

As we step out of darkness into Kingdom life, we may carry with us distorted images, either of ourselves or God, resulting from past experiences. When we are cut off from the perfect reflection of truth, our minds are filled with confusing perceptions. Our trouble begins when we accept the distortion as truth, rather than allow God to straighten us out.

When we come into Christ, we are a new creation that never existed before (2 Corinthians 5:17). We are starting fresh, learning a new way to live. How our original mind once thought has little impact on how we are called to live in the Kingdom. We have to begin by allowing Holy Spirit to build our identity on truth, getting rid of the distorted images and beliefs we previously based our lives on.

Before we were born again, we built mental and emotional walls out of every contorted brick thrown in our direction. Every humanistic thought, circumstance, struggle, and lie we believed were stacked one upon the other, cemented together with our own emotions and values, creating a place to be sabotaged from the inside by the forces of darkness. We ended up sustaining this wall that we thought was protecting us, when in reality, it was preventing us from finding transforming truth!

This life we are called to is less about getting into Heaven in the sweet by-and-by and more about transformation through our relationship with our Heavenly Father, who wants every part of us: spirit, mind, will, emotions, and body. He's all about our discovering who we are as His beloved children, as we look into *His* perfect mirror (His Word), seeing ourselves through Him, and adjusting ourselves to our new image.

Let's allow the perfected love of Holy Spirit to tear down the walls we have been hiding behind and fighting from. Then, we can be fully exposed to His light and fully healed so those distorted images are powerless against us. Now that we've come face-to-face with the truth, let's allow Holy Spirit to smash every contorted mirror and debilitating, toxic thoughts we've ever had.

Let's expose, through God's Word and our relationship with Jesus Christ, all that the Enemy has twisted and allow our Father to demolish strongholds and restore us to our original purpose in the likeness of Him!

GRAB YOUR JOURNAL!

What is God showing you at this moment?

In light of this revelation, how does this shift your thoughts and actions?

Tend To Your Seed

READ

Genesis 22:17-18,

Galatians 3:16,

Mark 4:3-20

Galatians 3:25-28,

Matthew 13:31,

Luke 17:21,

Luke 6:27-28,

Romans 2:4,

Hosea 10:12,

Proverbs 25:11,

Proverbs 25:15,

Proverbs 15:1-4,

Psalms 103:10-12,

2 Corinthians 5:21,

John 12:23-25,

James 4:1-10,

John 12:23-25,

Galatians 5:16-24

One morning, I woke up to an immediate resounding thought, "blessed to be a blessing." I thought of Abraham and how God promised all the nations of the earth would be blessed through his seed, Jesus Christ (Galatians 3:16). Through His death, burial (planting), and His resurrected life, He bore fruit in the form of all who have accepted God as Father! God *always* has a redemptive solution, and He has placed seed *in* us, then *planted us* on Earth to bless every life and situation we encounter.

In the natural, we plant seeds for the production of fruit to be consumed for nourishment, to produce shade, or to beautify an area. Planting is an act of faith with the plan to enjoy a harvest. Matthew 13:31 says the Kingdom of Heaven is like a seed, and Luke 17:21 says the kingdom is *in* us, so we are to plant seeds with Christ and the Kingdom in mind. Just as we plant apple seeds with our view toward an apple orchard, we plant seeds of the Kingdom "... with a view to righteousness [that righteousness, like seed, may germinate]..." (Hosea 10:12a AMP).

What we say and do are seeds to those in our realm of influence, and they produce after their kind, so we should plant only that which we want to reap a harvest because what we plant *will grow*! Seeds of condemnation reap rebellion. Seeds of accusation reap distance. Seeds of discord reap strife. On the contrary, gentle wisdom will overcome the strongest resistance (Proverbs 25:15) and soft answers turn away wrath (Proverbs 15:1).

Planting a seed means dying to immediate selfish motives to reap a future of peace. Christ planted in us brings us to life and reveals our purpose, and with love as our only motive, we consistently sow, water, weed, and nurture the garden of our heart. As we die to self by cultivating our relationship with Him, *The Seed* produces His righteousness.

Becoming frustrated towards loved ones who are in sin only drives them further away. Romans 2:4 says it is God's kindness that leads us to a new way of thinking. Jesus loved us before we were lovable. Doesn't Luke 6:27 encourage us to love, show kindness, and do good to those who just don't have it in them to love us back? Hebrews 12:11 tells us training and discipline produces a harvest of peace and righteousness. So if we tend our heart's garden, sowing love with our view toward righteousness, we're going to produce mature and irresistible fruit!

He is our *source of blessing*, and we are to *become like Him*, a living sacrifice; a seed *He* has planted, for nourishment, or shade from the heat to those whose lives we touch.

Let's tend to our seeds!

GRAB YOUR JOURNAL!

What is God showing you at this moment?

In light of this revelation, how does this shift your thoughts and actions?

Thoughts and Whispers

READ
Galatians 3:25-27,
2 Peter 1:1-12,
Proverbs 13:12,
Lamentations 3:22-23,
Hebrews 12:1-13,
Psalms 119:105

We all love those movies like *Rocky, Unbreakable*, or *Hacksaw Ridge*, where the hero rises up and succeeds after much adversity. There's something which connects our spirit with the hero's struggle, causing us to despise the villain and feel part of the victory! We cheer when evil is finally silenced, and justice is served! All the hero's failures and shortcomings pale in comparison to the reward. How easy it is to forget the trials that ushered in the victory.

So, why do we often sell ourselves short and beat ourselves up while we're still in the middle of our own story? None of us desire adversity, yet *here* it is, staring us in the face every day. Like the hero of the story, we come to many crossroads with sweat on our brows, wondering if *today* we will find the resolve to run well.

The *God of all creation* designed us for His glory, but our situations can seem less than glorious. God created us *on* purpose, *with* a purpose! But often, we are either unaware of it, fall short of it, or feel unworthy of it. So we stop short of our potential, *not* because of some great demonic force or a physical barrier but because of a thought or a whisper.

The Devil whispers in our ear we may as well give up trying to "be someone we're not," and we get weighed down in our walk. He may even use other's voices to delay our destiny. Insecure thoughts deceive us into thinking God is angry or disappointed in us, so our hope is deferred and our hearts break (Proverbs 13:12). We grieve when our past circumstance rears its ugly head again, yet we bow our knees to it over and over.

The Bible is a book of heroes whose lives testify God's faithfulness in the midst of failure, unfaithfulness, sickness, attack, and aborted missions. We have a God of unlimited patience (Lamentations 3:22-23). He is the greatest coach to have in our corner encouraging us in our fight!

Hebrews 12:1 (AMP, emphasis mine) says to strip off *every* unnecessary *weight* and the *sin* which *so easily and cleverly* entangles us (my paraphrase). Because of what Jesus endured to give us, let's keep our focus on His faithfulness. Let's strengthen our feeble knees, raise our weary hands, to blaze a path for our feet. Silence the whispers of the Enemy of our story by expressing glory to God for giving us one more day to wake up and *represent Him!* He will light our way through adversity, pain, and even our failures until we stand victorious before Him!

Our stories are *not over!*

GRAB YOUR JOURNAL! | *What is God showing you at this moment?*
| *In light of this revelation, how does this shift your thoughts and actions?*

Sewer Water or Living Water?

READ

Proverbs 13:12,

Psalms 1:1-6,

John 4:7-14,

Jeremiah 17:8,

John 7:37-38

Willow trees are beautiful to me. As a kid, I thought of them as fairy castles, so elegant and mysterious. We had one in our backyard at one point, planted close to a pond, and I told my dad it should be closer to the house. He said it was impossible because of their root system. The willow tree is a very thirsty tree with aggressive roots. He told me they are able to sense moisture in sewer and water lines and will try to crush them to get to the water. Without a plentiful water source, they will go after *anything* that provides moisture.

Like the willow tree, we were designed by God to need and have a constant plentiful supply of nourishment. We were made *by* Love, *for* love, and *to* love! We are meant for fellowship and union with Holy Spirit.

When we were cut off from God through Adam's sin, we were cut off from our *source* (Genesis 3). Since *God is love* (1 John 4:8), that means we were cut off from love. So, just like the tree grasping for water, even if it must take it from a sewer line, humanity searches for love and acceptance anywhere it can find it. People, in desperation to attain it, will go after anything resembling their idea of what love is, even if what they are drinking is polluted.

In desperation to receive, the insecure will hold tightly to any semblance of love, no matter how twisted it may be. Their grip can actually end up destroying the supplier or the relationship, as they discover their source is limited in supply and they experience a series of failed expectations.

No person can ever be responsible for the love only found in a relationship with the Heavenly Father, through Holy Spirit. If we are expecting someone outside of Christ to fulfill our need, we have already set them up for failure and condemned ourselves to disappointment. We have set that person up as God, and we are either okay or broken based on what they do.

When Jesus met the woman at the well in John 4, she had been married multiple times. Each relationship had most likely made her feel more and more insecure, seeking love and validation in the arms of men who could never truly provide it. I can only imagine the sting of rejection she must have felt. But, Jesus saw something different and offered her *Living Water*, an *eternal spring of life, identity*, and *love*! When He told her all she'd done, He changed the source where she drew "water."

We are going to become like the source we drink from. Holy Spirit shows us how to receive love from God and *become* love like Him so we are not *in need of* love from anyone else! As Christians, let's examine the source of our drinking water. Let's be careful of the things we meditate on, what we allow ourselves to believe, what we put in front of us, and how we entertain ourselves. Is what we chase satisfying us or pacifying us? Is it life-giving? Does it bring peace? Does it look like Jesus' life? Does it motivate and energize us?

Or, have we relegated ourselves to sucking sewer water, allowing polluted sources to rob us of our vision and energy—contaminating our destiny because we'll "take what we can *get*" rather than becoming what we were *created for*?

Proverbs 13:12 says when we have a deep desire, it is a tree of life to us. When we saturate ourselves in the *love of God*, He brings the fulfillment of joy and energy!

But, we won't get it by just wishing things would change. If His Word says we have been transplanted into His Kingdom, why allow our roots to cling to sewer lines?

Let's saturate ourselves in His life-giving, dream-inspiring, energizing love!

GRAB YOUR JOURNAL!

What is God showing you at this moment?

In light of this revelation, how does this shift your thoughts and actions?

Dancing in the Fire

READ

Daniel 3,

2 Corinthians 2:14,

Isaiah 55:7-13,

Proverbs 3:5-10,

Hebrews 13:8,

John 17

As a child, one of my favorite Bible stories was Shadrach, Meshach, and Abednego (especially the totally cool Veggie Tales version). I love their tenacity when they protested the king's command to bow to his idol and were condemned to die in a fiery furnace: "We have no need to answer you in this matter. Our God can deliver us, *but even if He doesn't*, we won't serve your gods or worship your image" (Daniel 3:16-18, my paraphrase).

But why didn't God just put the fire out or part the flames?

Could it be God wasn't threatened by the power of the fire and *chose* not to *honor* it? Could it be that He became *so excited* about the faith of His kids, He decided to dance in the flames with them? It was because He sustained them *in the fire*, He changed the hearts and minds of a king and nation!

We are going to face challenges which will try to uproot the planted Word. We are going to suffer loss in some form or fashion, whether it be a job, friends, personal failure, or even the death of a loved one. The challenge is keeping the flame of God so hot in our hearts that the fire around us is no competition!

We've been trained to pray for better circumstances, and when they don't happen right away, we live with a lot of failed expectations which bring discouragement. We question what we're doing wrong, if we need to pray better, why God's not listening, where God is in our lives, and what we did to open this door. That's humanistic thinking, not "God-in-me" thinking.

James 1:2-4 tells us to count it all joy when we fall into tough circumstances so Christ can be manifested through us, to bring us to the place where we lack nothing. We do not judge God based on what we're going through, continually putting His love on trial.

God is living in us, longing to reveal Himself *through* us, in the midst of trials and tribulations. He hasn't changed, and the reason we're alive hasn't changed —to be in a love relationship with God, love people, and manifest Christ as dear children.

A trusting relationship sounds like, "Father, You are my Lord, not these circumstances. All the answers are found in You. You close wrong doors and open right ones. I thank You for Your love, wisdom, provision, and favor. You didn't spare Your Son for my sake, so how will You not freely give me all I need? I know You will bring me to where I need to be in Your perfect timing."

This is so much better than feeling sorry for ourselves when things are not going according to "our" plan.

Causing us to triumph in His name means that He first wants us to see things differently. I'm not saying we shouldn't pray for blessing and favor. But, we need to recognize we are *in* the world not *of* the world. The *world* needs to see Christians go through earthly fire with the *fire of Holy Spirit* and the joyful anticipation of *good* burning in our hearts and peace in our minds!

GRAB YOUR JOURNAL! | *What is God showing you at this moment?*

In light of this revelation, how does this shift your thoughts and actions?

The Danger of Comparison

READ

Philippians 4:11-13 (AMP),

2 Corinthians 10:3-6,

Hebrews 6:19,

Galatians 6:7-9,

1 Corinthians 13:12,

Isaiah 40:28-31 (AMP),

Luke 6:45

Have you ever struggled in the area of comparison? If you've ever experienced sibling rivalry, asked, "Why me?", felt like you didn't fit in or measure up, sensed unfair treatment, tried to position your children for success and favor, or experienced unexpected loss, then the answer is a resounding *yes*! We constantly measure ourselves to certain standards; real or imagined.

The well-known scripture, "I can do all things through Christ which strengtheneth me," Philippians 4:13 (KJV) follows two verses which only take a moment to memorize but will be a continual learning process to live out. Paul wrote that he had learned in whatever position he found himself in to be *content*. He knew *how* to be humble, to live prosperously, to be full *or* hungry, to suffer need, and to abound. Persecution or trials can either strengthen us or bury us. How we handle abundance and prosperity will reveal if money or God rules our hearts.

If you haven't already figured this out, life is not fair. Sometimes bad things happen for no other reason than Satan is a jerk, on the move to seek, kill, and destroy. But God is not the author of death nor destruction. He is sovereign over all, wise in His decisions, loves and cares for all in need. We live in a fallen world, and it is better to live trusting the Sovereign and Good Father than to fall into bitter comparison. The answer is never that God is unfairly punishing you, and we should never give in to the pressure to provide an answer that will never be good enough.

Many times, what we're going through is more important to us than who we are becoming. Too often, we blame God for our situations because it's easier to get ticked off, escape, or lower our expectations than it is to take charge of our thoughts, faith, and actions. I often wonder if I've actually prolonged certain circumstances because of the thoughts I failed to take captive and subject to God's Word, allowing my mouth to reveal what was in my heart in abundance (Luke 6:45).

Galatians 6:7 says God won't be mocked, and whatever we sow, we're going to reap. If we sow to our *flesh*, what we reap will eventually come to ruin. But, if we sow to our *spirit*, we reap something life-giving which is eternal. We can't allow ourselves to become weary in doing good, fueling *deceptive thoughts* and attitudes which rob us of hope or *disruptive thoughts* which pull us away from our faith!

Let's take a minute and examine the areas of our lives where we've been struggling with comparison and attitudes we've left unchecked. Let's repent of allowing discord to interrupt our faith to change our situation. Let's invite God to show Himself strong on our behalf through worship and make a public display against the enemy. Let's sow to our spirit, so, like Paul, we may know that regardless of our situation, we have contentment beyond human reasoning.

GRAB YOUR JOURNAL!

What is God showing you at this moment?

In light of this revelation, how does this shift your thoughts and actions?

Divine Connection to a Framing Nailer

READ
Isaiah 62:5,
Jeremiah 2:32,
John 17
(Jesus' prayer for us),
Ephesians 5:25-33,
Matthew 7:21-23,
2 Timothy 3:5-7,
Acts 1:4-8

You'll never know why people get a "rush" over using power tools until you've experienced it for yourself. If you've never experienced the thrill of firing a framing nail gun powered by compressed air, you're missing out!

It was an essential tool in building a wrap-around porch on our house. A nail gun can shoot ten nails in the time it takes me to drive one nail with a hammer. The secret to this awesome tool is a few drops of oil where the tool connects to the hose and a large tank of air powered by a motor.

Without the oil, the nails can get hung up and malfunction, causing wear and tear on the components and potential corrosion. Without the air compressor tank, the nail gun is just a visually impressive but powerless tool. Without these essential components, it is entirely useless to the builder.

As Christians, we may serve God and be sincere in our beliefs. We may even look impressive, like the framing nail gun, but without the oil of anointing and our divine connection, the breath of His Spirit, we are powerless.

Unlike the framing nailer, however, we are *not* just tools in the hand of the Builder. If you're like me, you're a *doer*; sometimes it's hard to simply sit and connect deeply. I *want* connection; I want to be "used" by God. But, He doesn't just want to have a "business connection" with us. Without relationship with Him through Holy Spirit, we reduce Christianity to mere servanthood.

It took almost two years of weekends for my husband and I to build our porch. It was tough. There were days we felt like doing other things. But, we were dedicated to each other *and* to our goal. My husband never lorded over me, and it was my pleasure and joy to *work with him*. We work well together *because* of our relationship.

As we are the bride of Christ, we are privileged to work with Him side-by-side, enjoying relationship as we build something together, benefitting from the joy of simply being with each other. When we understand we are one *together*, two hearts united, loving those He loves, we become effective in ministry, miracles, and purpose.

GRAB YOUR JOURNAL!

What is God showing you at this moment?

In light of this revelation, how does this shift your thoughts and actions?

Memorial Day Celebration

READ

John 3:16-17,

John 15:12-17,

Hebrews 12:1-3,

Romans 12:1-2 (AMP),

Romans 5:17-21,

Romans 6,

Matthew 5:16

Growing up in military towns allows people to see things differently than in other places. We see the convoys on the road, the camouflaged uniforms of soldiers on their way to work, the many retired war dogs who proudly wear their veterans ball caps, and our military museums and memorials. We have no problems with large displays of patriotism or American flags. We *love* our military men and women and typically can't understand why some disdain the military that protects the very freedoms they enjoy.

However you choose to celebrate any of our patriotic holidays, whether at a church service, museum, beach, or barbecue, take some time to remember those who paid the ultimate price; who gave us these freedoms to enjoy. It was their honor and privilege to sacrifice so future generations could be free.

As Christians, we also acknowledge the ultimate sacrifice of our Heavenly Father who gave us His Son, Jesus, who laid down *His life* for us, so we may find it. It was His pleasure to do so because His reward is those who believe!

We never want to grieve Holy Spirit by walking in less than what His sacrifice paid to reveal. That's why we must search out the benefits of our salvation. Salvation is not just a ticket to Heaven, and we don't just *add* Him to our lives. Instead, we live a life of sacrifice toward God which is loaded with benefits (Psalms 103).

As we submit to Holy Spirit, we learn to *explore by faith* this *new* life as we walk away from our dead self. To intentionally live less than what Jesus paid for is the same as rejecting a costly gift from a beloved friend. When we explore the presence, power, and the call of God in our lives, we honor Him. Proverbs

25:2 (AMP) says, "It is the glory of God to conceal a matter, But the glory of kings is to search out a matter."

Revelation through relationship is layered upon God's Word, and He is a *rewarder* of those who *diligently* seek Him. As we seek Him, stepping out in faith, sharing His gospel, or healing the sick, He expands our revelation. As we are drawn deeper, He increases our revelation of freedom, and we learn the joy of loving beyond our comfort zone. We honor His sacrifice and see His name glorified.

Let's celebrate by exploring His gift of everlasting life without self-imposed limits that keep us from fully trusting this God who gave *everything*. Let's celebrate every day, honoring what His Son's blood paid for on the cross! We are *redeemed and free*!

GRAB YOUR JOURNAL!

What is God showing you at this moment?

In light of this revelation, how does this shift your thoughts and actions?

Unanswered Prayers

READ

Psalms 144:1-2,

1 Timothy 6:12,

James 1:4,

2 Timothy 4:7,

Matthew 6:10,

Matthew 8:17,

Psalms 103:2-4,

Hebrews 4:9-16,

Isaiah 53:5,

3 John 1:2,

2 Corinthians 8:2,

John 10:10,

Isaiah 50:7,

Proverbs 10:22,

James 1:4

I heard an interesting sermon about "prayers that have *yet* to be answered," and I'm still chewing on it. Not only does it leave me with an unsettling conviction but also a peace about working through this journey. I still wrestle in certain areas to enter into the *rest* of faith (Hebrews 4:11), but that *is* the "good fight" (1 Timothy 6:12).

There is no instruction about unanswered prayer, but that doesn't mean there are no delays or processes. There are questions we have and destinations in prayer where we can see the ultimate answer, but God may be incorporating something deeper into that answer. So, we must *traverse* the path, praying into His will, so the answer will be perfect, complete, and lacking nothing (James 1:4).

Prayer isn't trying to get God to change His mind. Psalms 144:1-2 says He's the one who gives me strength and skill for the battle. He wants us to fight alongside Him, against principalities that are working against what we're fighting for. If God is *leading us* into the battle, we can rest assured He intends to come away with a victory. We don't have to manipulate God, people, or circumstances but rather respond to the invitation to come boldly to the throne and have conversations which bring about change.

Although our desire is to see God do miracles, it's not our job to make excuses for why they don't happen when or how we wanted it to. I believe 3 John 1:2 conveys the heart of God for us: is above all things we are in good health. Since Jesus bore our sicknesses on the cross, I don't think we should ever sanctify something He suffered to get rid of (Isaiah 53:4-5). While we know that in all things God works for the good of those who love him (Romans 8:28), I do not believe we should accept sickness as something God gives to build character in us. Will He use it? Absolutely. Did He give it? I do not believe so. Giving people sickness goes against everything Jesus taught and modeled.

We plant our feet, set our jaw, and refuse to lose faith when *what* we are praying for *aligns* with God's Word. If our prayers are self-pity in disguise, we're just looking for relief without maturity. He wants us to grow up in our faith and become seasoned warriors. He wants not only the miracle at the moment but relationship with everyone it influences. He wants our hearts.

Let's *re*calibrate our hearts and minds so we may act as partners with God. Let's deny ourselves the right to function in fear, doubt, blame, and discouragement. Let's pursue God for our role in the miracle; whether fasting, praying without ceasing, speaking what God is saying, or contending with a stronghold that is refusing to move. I don't believe we should assume an unanswered prayer is God's sovereignty. If something happens contrary to our prayer, may it push us *further* into the throne room of Heaven until we find our answers or lean into the mystery. Let our *first* priority be to be His intimate partner, surrendering to His ways, and bringing His Kingdom wherever we go.

It's time to see *His Kingdom* come and *His* will be done on earth as it is in Heaven.

GRAB YOUR JOURNAL! | *What is God showing you at this moment?*

In light of this revelation, how does this shift your thoughts and actions?

How to Be Angry and Sin Not

READ

Ephesians 4:1-32,

John 8:1-11,

2 Corinthians 5:11-21,

Mark 6:34,

2 Corinthians 4:4,

John 8:3-12

My father-in-law used to say of people who stirred up trouble, "They are muddyin' up the water in my pond." Our water of life was clear and calm until that person blew in like a hurricane, and our attitude was blown to pieces for a time. We may have even found the mention of their name made us a little angry.

We may have felt we had the right to tell that person off, speak our mind, or act out in anger, but all that does is sear our hearts, burn bridges, and cause our witness to be called into question. It may feel cathartic in the moment, but deep down, we know it brings a sense of separation.

So, how can we be "... angry and sin not" (Ephesians 4:26 KJV)?

We must realize, even if it seems this way, people are not our enemy. We must ask God to change our hearts to see their created value. We confront the lie perpetuating deception by Satan who has blinded them to the truth. If they still disdain us, it won't be for our anger or condemnation. They are just not ready to see light. Until then, keep loving, keep planting, keep praying.

In John 8, the Pharisees tried to muddy the waters by tricking Jesus into error to disqualify Him in the eyes of the people, so they brought a woman caught in adultery to where Jesus was teaching. The law said she must be put to death by stoning. If He went against the law, He'd be considered a false prophet. If He stoned her, His compassion would be called into question. Knowing their hearts, Jesus said, "He that is without sin among you, let him first cast a stone at her" (John 8:7 KJV). With one statement, not only did He disqualify them but qualified Himself to stone her, but He would not! So, what I'm understanding Him to say is, "I don't accuse you, because I don't see you for what you've *done* but who you are created to *be*. I see the lies you've believed about yourself

58

and your search for peace and acceptance to fill the emptiness of your life. I'm here to show you that you don't have to continue to look in all the wrong places, but see how precious you are to God!"

When we begin to see people through Christ's eyes, as sheep without a shepherd, blind and stumbling, we'll no longer judge according to the flesh (2 Corinthians 5:16). We'll see them as God's children, created for His purpose, having been alienated through deception or offense. This makes them easier to love and pray for if we see them as terrorized victims of a relentless Devil. Then, we can aim righteous anger at the *real* enemy.

God *is Love*, and *Love* is our most powerful weapon. Faith works through love. He has given us authority over wickedness and rulers of darkness. Let's begin to take authority over the forces which blind men from seeing God's glory! Let's, instead, call them *out of darkness* and *into His marvelous light*, never permitting sin against us to create sin inside us! Let's allow the peace of God to reign in our hearts and clear those muddy waters.

GRAB YOUR JOURNAL! | *What is God showing you at this moment?*

In light of this revelation, how does this shift your thoughts and actions?

Free Indeed!

READ

John 8:31-47,

James 4:1-10,

Hebrews 6:19,

Hebrews 12:1,

Galatians 2:20-21,

Galatians 5,

Galatians 3:25-29,

1 Corinthians 10:22-24,

Acts 17:28

When Jesus preached on true freedom in John 8, the Pharisees confronted Him saying in verse 33 (AMP), "We are Abraham's descendants and have never been enslaved to anyone." Yet, all the while, they were under the tyranny of Roman rule. They were deceived into believing as long as they had the freedom to maintain their own religious practices and lord over their own people, they were free of oppression themselves.

To the world, the ability to do whatever the flesh desires *is* freedom, so people find themselves raging against anyone who seeks to impede them, *not realizing* they are slaves to every whim. They have no hope to anchor them, so their freedom is only relative to their ever-changing emotional state. It's easier to blame social or racial injustice, government, family members, or employers for their lack of peace or condition than to challenge their thoughts or hold them up to the light of God's Word.

True freedom starts within the heart by *dying to one's self* and becoming *alive in Christ* (Galatians 2:20). It is found in the heart *only* when Holy Spirit resides within. It is an identity of sonship to Creator God, bought for us through the gift of salvation through our resurrection by Christ Jesus. I love something Pastor Candace Carle, my pastor's daughter, once said that has stuck with me, "*Who* I am is found *in the I am.*"

Once our identity is *established* as a *beloved child of God*, every action we take or thought we entertain and allow to grow, comes from Heaven towards earth as water to dry ground. If we never grasp *this identity*, we will see ourselves cut off from our eternal supply in Christ, slaves of our circumstances. We will be striving against the world in an attempt to gain favor with God to receive from

Him, yet we will be no better than the world we think we are free from.

When we are born again, our hearts become one with His, and we take on His characteristics and values. We're not controlled by a disciplinarian with a list of the do's and don'ts. His Kingdom is boundless, and He wants to show us the expanse of it. God doesn't want us entangled with yokes of bondage that easily ensnare us. The Apostle Paul, in writing about breaking away from certain religious practices in 1 Corinthians 10:23 said, even if all things are morally legitimate, they're not always advantageous or edifying to spiritual life. We see it is in Him; *we live, function, and have our identity* (Acts 17:28 TPT)!

When our hearts understand the revelation that we are *truly free*, we don't have to work so hard to convince our head.

GRAB YOUR JOURNAL! | *What is God showing you at this moment?*

In light of this revelation, how does this shift your thoughts and actions?

How Big is Our God?

READ

2 Corinthians 10:2-7,

Psalms 23:4-6,

Matthew 8:23-34,

Philippians 1,

Matthew 6:10,

Philippians 1:21,

Mark 4:35-41,

Acts 20:34

I had a conversation with someone who had experienced a weightiness in their spirit after visiting a city. She said she could feel the spiritual oppression there and was burdened by the lack of God's presence. Wrestling with grief, she didn't know what to do. Before I could even formulate the thought, I knew the answer.

Being a born-again believer, she was picking up on the heart of God for the city, but the filter of her emotions clouded her discernment. Instead of releasing the city to Holy Spirit, she had been robbed of sleep because of worry.

2 Corinthians 10:5b (TPT, emphasis added) says, "We capture, like prisoners of war, every thought and *insist* that it bow in obedience to the Anointed One." We must quiet those storms in our hearts and minds and focus on being Spirit led rather than emotionally driven or led by the ways of the world.

If we can sense the atmosphere in a room of people, could it be we can sense the feelings of the demonic spirits who are assigned to a certain region? Maybe when we are sensing anxiety and fear, it's that of the Enemy, aware of Christ in us. Maybe we need to be more aware of Christ in us (He never leaves nor forsakes us) than we are of the darkness around us.

In Mark 4:35-41, Jesus went with His disciples into a storm He could sleep through. In Matthew 8:28-34, a demon-possessed man, sensing the presence of Jesus, fell at His feet in fear, pleading not to be tormented before their time. In Acts 20:23, The Holy Spirit led Paul into town after town where prisons and tribulation were waiting for him. But because *he didn't value his own life*, he went *without fear*, knowing to live is Christ, but in death there was *more to gain*.

Before we start sizing-up our situations, maybe we should size-up the God we worship. Before we start discerning the spiritual condition of the places we go, let's take time to discern the love our Father has for us and where He has sent us to *represent* Jesus. Rather than talking about our fears and feelings and casting judgements with our tongue, let's surrender to Holy Spirit's lead, asking Him what to pray and speak into the atmosphere which opens the door for His Kingdom to manifest on Earth!

GRAB YOUR JOURNAL!

What is God showing you at this moment?

In light of this revelation, how does this shift your thoughts and actions?

Reminders of His Presence

READ

Hebrews 13:5,

Isaiah 26:3,

I Chronicles 4:9-10,

Psalms 23,

Joshua 1:3-9,

Genesis 15:5-6

Have there been times in your life when you just *knew* God was with you? Maybe there was a time when you had to *fully* rely on Him and sensed Holy Spirit was almost standing beside you. It's as if, without saying a word, His presence brought a sense of peace which made every question disappear and every anxiety cease. Nothing had externally changed, but the earthquake in your mind simply stopped.

In truth, He is always *that* close. Hebrews 13:5 (AMP) says, "I will never [under any circumstances] desert you [nor give you up nor leave you without support, nor will I in any degree leave you helpless], nor will I forsake nor let you down or relax My hold on you [assuredly not]!"

However, there are times we're unaware of His presence. We never intentionally leave God out, but we live in a very distracting world, and things seem to pile up in front of us. Sometimes we subconsciously think, "I got this," or, "I don't need help with this because it's logical," and we forget He may just may have some input. We develop areas of expertise like things we've been trained to do in our job or an activity or hobby which we've perfected by practice. We look at these as things we know well, so we don't have to ask for God's help. They're simple.

But, God is interested in making the mundane parts of our lives part of His mission even if we're only pumping gas or grocery shopping. He delights in giving us ideas that will prosper us in our hearts and lives which, in turn, bring glory to His Name.

Just as God showed Abraham a nightly reminder of His promise when he looked at the stars, I have set up times of awareness to settle my mind, and prompt me to remember God is with me. If I'm in the car alone, I worship. When I look in a mirror, I thank Him for living in the person staring back at me. It's a sticky note on my computer at work or anything which brings focus and peace when my mind goes off on some tangent because the day isn't going as planned. I want to be brought back to God, to His peace.

Let's practice the *awareness* that God is with us *all the time*, listening to every conversation, waiting to interject. Let's look for Him to show up in everything we do. When we're focused on Him and His love for us, we become kingdom minded, looking for ways to manifest His presence and bring glory to God!

GRAB YOUR JOURNAL!

What is God showing you at this moment?

In light of this revelation, how does this shift your thoughts and actions?

One Decision, Many Victories

READ

Proverbs 4:1-13,

Romans 8:5-39,

Esther 4:14,

John 16:33,

Hebrews 12:2,

Psalms 144:1-2

There is an interesting story about a thirty-four-year-old school teacher, Joshua Chamberlain. He was a volunteer Union soldier during the Civil War, who made *one decision*, resulting in the turning point at Gettysburg which won the war, making our country the *United* States of America.

Joshua Chamberlain was a school teacher, but in spite of having *no* military training, was given the rank of Lieutenant Colonel and stationed at Gettysburg. He was told the Confederacy would win the war within months if they took the hill. He began with 1,000 men, but by the second day, was down to 300. By the rebel's fifth charge up the hill, they were down to only eighty, having used all the ammunition from the dead and wounded.

When his lookout saw the enemy regrouping, everyone looked to him. How easy it would have been to retreat. Instead, he commanded his men to affix bayonets! Joshua Chamberlain changed the course of history with one decision to foolishly charge the enemy with little ammunition. However, he didn't know the enemy, who outnumbered them, was also low on bullets. They hoped to intimidate the haggard forces of the Confederacy. When Chamberlain charged, the rebels turned and ran, thinking they had misjudged the opposition's strength and number.

The battle of Gettysburg was pivotal in the success of the war. If Chamberlain had lost, the South would have had the advantage, and some believe America would not just have been divided into North and South but several smaller countries. We would not have had the power to defeat Hitler or Japan nor to become a stabilizing force in our present day.[5] America is the longest-tenured government in history. There are countries older than we are but not a continuous form of government, all because of one school teacher who made one decision 150 years ago. He wouldn't live long enough to see the result of his decision, but he has impacted every life on the planet.

We were given an assignment by God, often placed in positions we don't feel qualified for. Battles are a part of life, but Holy Spirit is in us to teach us how to fight (Psalms 144:1-2). We should never underestimate our position. Whether we see the results of our decision to face the hard times or not, our battle may be a part of someone else's victory. How we respond to the challenges we face matters, and the decisions we do or don't make impacts those around us. A kind word in due season, an act of compassion, or a listening ear to a hurting soul just may be enough of a seed that will change someone's outlook on life or the gospel.

Check out this humorous segment from Andy Andrews' video on this subject on YouTube: Andy Andrews: There Would Be No USA if...(Life Today/James Robinson) https://www.youtube.com/watch?v=5712EECFzTA

GRAB YOUR JOURNAL!

What is God showing you at this moment?

In light of this revelation, how does this shift your thoughts and actions?

Let Truth Set You Free!

READ

Romans 7:15-8:16,

Philippians 3:12-14,

John 8:36,

Matthew 6:19-23,

Psalms 119:105-112 (TPT)

How often do we attach labels to ourselves or others? We tend to judge according to what we see. If we don't like a few extra pounds we see in the mirror, we can judge ourselves as failures. A child who has given up in school because they struggle might be seen as lazy. We may judge our parenting skills if our child goes astray. We sometimes judge ourselves as unrighteous because we struggle in an area we believe to be powerless to change.

If we're not careful, we will allow life to speak louder than God's Word and become the judge and jury of our own heart. We should never drag our dead past into our living present, even if it was thirty seconds ago. If we err, we should immediately repent by running to the lap of our Daddy God, and thanking Him for who we are to *Him*, and how He paid such a *high price* to *live* in us!

We can now have a clean conscience because Holy Spirit gives us the ability to separate who we are from the things we have done and the labels we have given ourselves. If we sin, we have the ability to repent, which means we see it *through* the *light* of *truth* which sets us free.

We have to quit looking at what we did, or what has been done to us, and start looking at what we're becoming in Christ! The only way to do this is to get alone with God, stop trying to be accepted by the world, and just enjoy His acceptance. Declare He is *true* and has saved us, His *favor* is upon us, and we are His dear children!

We tend to pray about troubles and how to make our days go better. We tape scriptures around the house (not a bad thing to do), hoping they will help us "do" better. But, if we do this at the expense of ignoring *our identity* in Christ, then *life* becomes our barometer instead of *Christ above all.*

Subsequently, we find ourselves in constant need of prayer or a dynamic worship service to get us pumped up again! Rather, our fuel should come from who He is in us and who we are in Him! When we look in the mirror, we should see a *child of God*, made in our Father's likeness, knowing He who is in us will never leave nor forsake us!

If our *eyes are focused* on *Him*, our entire body is flooded with *light*! We won't be drawn to what "feels right," bowing to human reasoning and drawn into darkness. If our eye is darkened by having our attention focused elsewhere, how twisted is our view? How dark is that darkness?

God's Word is a lamp unto our feet and a light to our path. Instead of looking at how far we have to go, let's see we have *somewhere* to go, follow the light of truth, and let *truth* bring us into freedom!

GRAB YOUR JOURNAL!

What is God showing you at this moment?

In light of this revelation, how does this shift your thoughts and actions?

It is Well With My Soul

READ

Romans 3:21-26,

James 2:14-26,

Ephesians 2:6-7,

1 Corinthians 13:1-3,

1 John 4:7-8,

Matthew 7:21-23,

1 John 2:1-29 (AMP),

Romans 8:1

A few years ago, an elderly man at my mother-in-law's church approached me and asked if I would sing at his funeral. We laughed as I told him not to go anywhere too soon, but I would be honored. When he passed, just short of ninety-one years old, I sang my favorite hymn, "It is Well," with my husband accompanying me on the piano.

During the funeral, one of his grandsons gave his grandfather's testimony. Lester Carter Jr. had been in church his entire life, taught Sunday School, was on the deacon board, and did his best to live "right" in the public eye. But on September 15, 1971, at forty-six years old, he had a heart attack. As he lay alone in his hospital bed, God spoke to his heart. Realizing he had never submitted his life to Christ as Savior, the truth set in that he would spend eternity in hell, and fear gripped him, but only for a moment. As he surrendered his life to Christ, light flooded his heart and mind. He was not only born again but delivered from alcoholism and his marriage rekindled. Having been given a second chance, he spent the rest of his career as a lawyer and judge, boldly sharing to anyone who would listen to the power of salvation, how Christ changed his life, and ministering to downtrodden men suffering from addiction.

How is it we can go through life putting ourselves through self-imposed tests where we are the one giving the grade? We can do something well and believe we deserve favor with God or punish ourselves when we commit a sin. If we live by our senses, we try to make our good outweighs our bad to "feel" justified.

1 Corinthians 13:1-3 says that we could give to the poor, give our bodies to be burned as sacrifice, and even have mountain moving faith, yet *without love*, (and God is Love), it means nothing. We don't want to stand before Him and

boast of all we've done in His Name, only to hear Him say, "I never *knew* you: depart from me" (Matthew 7:23a KJV, emphasis added).

At the same time, God holds no sin against us when we submit our lives to Him. He loves us unconditionally. He teaches us the way to walk (1 John 2:20), keeps us free from condemning thoughts (Romans 8:1), changes our hearts, and renews our minds as we spend time in His presence!

Before we're born again, everything we do is, at most, a good attempt which always falls short (Romans 3:23). As long as we are living by our senses, we are struggling to "be," struggling to earn the gift which has already been paid for and given to us. It is only after we put our faith in Jesus and Holy Spirit makes His home in us that eternity dwells in us. After that, everything we do is an extension of Who and what is inside of us. *Seated with Christ* in heavenly places (Ephesians 2:6-7), we are completely empowered because what we do is flowing through us from the heart of God, and *He* never falls short.

Let's keep our hearts submitted to our Father, receiving and being transformed by His grace, so we are assured, like the song says, "... My sin, not in part, but the whole, was nailed to the cross, and I bear it no more. Praise the Lord! It is well with my soul!"

GRAB YOUR JOURNAL!

What is God showing you at this moment?

In light of this revelation, how does this shift your thoughts and actions?

Be a Believing Believer

READ

2 Corinthians 10:4-6,

Matthew 11:12,

Galatians 5:6,

Proverbs 4:23,

Hebrews 4:16,

Romans 5:1,

Romans 1:17,

Galatians 3:11,

Hebrews 10:38

Have you ever been around unbelieving believers? They accept Jesus for salvation but live as if they are without a Father. They respond like the world, to the news, tragedy, trials, and cultural conventions, either living passively without real interest or participation in God's will or becoming angry at Him for allowing things.

Chances are, we still have some areas where we're not walking with Him, even if we don't know it. We become more conscious of the Devil around us than the God within us.

When this happens, without realizing it, we've bowed to the subtle voice of the liar which tempts us to try to fix a problem in our own strength and our own knowledge. We may even take advice, even good advice from others before we take the time to listen to God. We can walk into our day unprepared for the "unexpecteds" which pop up to steal the Word from our hearts.

The constant renewal of our minds is part of the growing process. But, more than we need someone to pray for us because we fell prey to a lie, we need to replace those lies with truth, becoming aware of the weapons Holy Spirit has placed in our arsenal and how they work.

2 Corinthians 10 says our weapons are mighty in God for pulling down strongholds. But, a weapon is no good to us if we don't know how and when to use it. Whether strongholds are in our minds or over a city, our victory is in submission to God *through faith*.

By *deliberately submitting our thoughts* to the knowledge of God, the liar is resisted. As we *violently* cast down opposing thoughts, we *passionately* draw on faith in God's Word. Matthew 11:12 says the kingdom of heaven is taken by *violence*, but I prefer the Passion Translation, "The realm of heaven's kingdom is *bursting forth*, and *passionate* people have *taken hold* of its power" (Matthew 11:12 TPT, emphasis added).

Our victory *is faith*. We are justified by it, live by it, and it *works through love*. Without love, faith has no door to walk through, nothing to cling to. Life comes at us fast, and we can't sell so quickly what Jesus, our Lord, paid such a high price to dwell in our hearts (Proverbs 4:23). Faith gives us confidence to the throne of grace (Hebrews 4:16).

Let's start distrusting our doubts, calling the Enemy out on his lies by reminding him about what God has said. Let's hold fast to our profession of faith in the midst of all the Enemy does to wrestle it out of our hearts. Let's be believing believers!

GRAB YOUR JOURNAL!

What is God showing you at this moment?

In light of this revelation, how does this shift your thoughts and actions?

Far From Oppression

READ

Proverbs 23:7,

Colossians 2:6-9,

Isaiah 54:10-17,

Colossians 3:3,

Ephesians 6:10-18,

Revelation 12:11

I saw a meme on Facebook of a certain actor whose net worth is said to be well over $200 million, who was quoted as saying he was "tired of being oppressed." When I first read it, I laughed, but instantly, God quickened me, "He *is* oppressed." Though I really couldn't see how, I know better than to tell God He's wrong. So when I pressed in, he reminded me, "For as he thinks within himself, so is he" (Proverbs 23:7 TPT). Though this man lives a charmed life by my standards, his experience dictates how he sees himself, and no amount of money or fame can fix what God can.

Jesus told His disciples to be careful of the leaven of the Pharisees and of Herod (Mark 8:15). Leaven is a tiny but vital ingredient used in bread to make it rise. There are many little voices impacting our thought life, trying to tell us who we *are* based on our station in life, our race, our gender, our politics, our finances, or our past.

If we allow those voices to work their way in, they will create a lesser identity than our created value because it's *easier* to give in. When those accommodations become our standard, we prove life is all about what's in it for *us, our* blessing, and *our* problems rather than dying to "self," and manifesting what we say we believe in the middle of persecution. We allow what we *perceive* to have a louder voice than the God we say we serve.

When *Jesus* is at the center of our thoughts, our motivations, and our actions, we become rooted and grounded in *love*! Isaiah 54 says when we are established in righteousness (which we are *made* righteous in Christ), that we would be far from *even the thought of oppression*. He goes on to say, those who would stir up strife toward us will fall and surrender to us.

Revelation 12:11 says we *overcome our enemy* through the words of our mouth, the blood of the Lamb, *and* by *loving not our own lives unto death.* Attacks are going to come, but we can have undisturbed peace in the midst of them because we *know Whose we are.* Because Christ died, when righteous, when we are loved and in love with Jesus, we become *dead* to sin and alive in Christ. Sin loses its appeal because we're in love, so no weapon formed against us (and weapons *are* formed every day) shall prosper. Why? Because you can't kill a *dead* man!

God has a purpose and a plan for each of our lives and never runs out of ways to get us there, no matter how many times we've been detoured or gone our own ways. Like an internal GPS, He will continually reroute us to our destination. Nothing, or no one, can separate us from *His love*! And if *He* is for us, who can successfully stand against us? Our battle is not with flesh and blood. The battle is between our ears. The closer we are to righteousness, the further we are from even the *thought* of oppression. Whose voice deserves to dictate our destiny and establish our identity?

GRAB YOUR JOURNAL!

What is God showing you at this moment?

In light of this revelation, how does this shift your thoughts and actions?

Are You Holding Peace While Holding Your Peace?

READ

Exodus 14:13-15,

Proverbs 4:23,

Matthew 10:12-13 (TPT),

James 4:1-3,

Colossians 3:15 (AMPC),

James 1:19-27,

Proverbs 15:1,

John 14:26-28 (AMP),

Revelation 12:11

My adult daughter came home to live with us after her five year stint in the Marine Corps. She returned to attend college, and we are so happy she did! There have been some big adjustments on all of our parts due to having to share spaces again. Honestly, she would do anything for us with no thought of repayment. A child moved out, but a woman came back. It can be uncomfortable for her, not feeling like this is her own home. There have been times I've asked her to do a kitchen chore while I'm at work, only to come home and be disappointed, even if she'd been busy with other things all day.

However, rather than ask why, I'd "climb on the mom-cross" and begin cleaning the kitchen so I could make dinner. I'd breathe a heavy sigh, hoping she'd respond, rehearsing in my head what I'm *not* going to say, which is my passive-aggressive tendency. And while a lot more holding of the tongue is needed in this world, the reason for *holding our peace* should be because we *are holding peace*.

When Moses was backed up against the Red Sea with the Egyptian army bearing down on them, he told the people to *"hold their peace"* because he knew God had a plan. He was firmly confident in his heart and mind. There was no doubt or distress (Exodus 14:13-15).

If peace is not the reason behind our silence, then there's something off-kilter in our hearts and we need to address it. If, in our effort to avoid direct conflict, we suffer in silence, our hearts will find a way to reveal itself, whether through snide comments, silent treatments, or body language. *Our discipline to practice is to be quick to hear, slow to speak, and slow to anger (James 1:19).*

God showed me deception *starts* with a seed of offense. In my effort to avoid confrontation and conflict, when things needed to be addressed, I was actually building *offense in my heart which* could eventually skew the lens through which I see my daughter, the way I feel, and divide a beautiful relationship, over what *started out* as an unwashed dish.

Colossians 3:15 (AMPC) tells us to let *peace* be the *umpire of the soul*. Just like in baseball, this "ump" is making the calls we may want to argue with, but it can spot a strike from a mile away. Even if we are *right*, our hearts will condemn us if our thoughts are selfish.

If we are intentional about growing in Christ, let's *not avoid* the little things that can become big things if left unchecked. Let's not deceive ourselves being hearers and not doers. And while we do *well* to hold our tongues, let's make sure that the source of our silence is peace and that we remain uncontaminated by secular thought, comparison, pride, and selfishness.

GRAB YOUR JOURNAL!

What is God showing you at this moment?

In light of this revelation, how does this shift your thoughts and actions?

Wisdom, The Hearing Heart

READ

Romans 10:17,

1 Kings 3:5-12,

Mark 4:23-25,

2 Timothy 1:7,

Luke 8:18,

Philippians 4:8,

Romans 8:26-38

When God asked Solomon what He could give him, Solomon didn't exactly state, "Give me wisdom." He said, "... give Your servant an understanding mind *and* a hearing heart to judge Your people, that I may discern between good and bad" (1 Kings 3:9 AMPC). This request revealed Solomon's heart, and God saw his priorities were in the right place. Had Solomon selfishly asked for riches, long life, or the death of his enemies, he may have short-sightedly devalued his created purpose.

We all have mental or emotional filters which cause us to hear things in certain ways. For example, if you had a judgmental or hateful earthly father, it may cause you to misjudge *Father* God, and hold feelings of condemnation, judgment, or fear. A good doctor would never simply give us medicine for a fever caused by cancer. The fever is a symptom of the cancer, so he goes after the *source* of the fever. In the same way, God, our Great Physician, isn't merely after *relief* from a problem. Instead, He is going to the root of our thoughts to renew our minds and heal our hearts.

Mark 4:23-25 says we receive according to *how we measure* what we hear. A humble and teachable heart will receive so much more than someone who thinks they have it all figured out. Proud minds will devalue God's words, inching them further from the Truth, resulting in Satan stealing even more from their understanding. In contrast, the humble may hear a word with their heart, long before they understand it with their head. Though they may not be able to explain it, *life* is blown into their heart, seeing revelation which is God-breathed. It *won't* be stolen away!

Our belief systems are inadvertently shaped by whatever we give most of our attention to. If we take our eyes off Christ, we'll fall prey to attempting to level the playing field by lowering one standard to elevate another in the name of equality or justice, inviting a spirit of division. If we adjust our faith level to accommodate our emotions or circumstances, we may be comforted for a moment, but it will eventually cause us to build a barrier between us and God.

Romans 10:17(NKJV) says, "So then faith comes by *hearing*, and hearing by the word of God." In order to reshape our thinking, we must hear with the *right* mind, flooding our eyes and ears by reading, meditating, and speaking His Word.

Let's take a step back from what we *think we know* and how mature we *think* we are and receive, like a child, with humility and wonder. Let's hold our opinions up to the light of God's Word and examine them accordingly. Let's build faith that works for our good! For it is in that place we find room to grow and learn on a sure foundation. As His words become valuable and precious to us, we will find a place in His presence where we become a little more like Him every day.

GRAB YOUR JOURNAL!

What is God showing you at this moment?

In light of this revelation, how does this shift your thoughts and actions?

You Need a Bath!

READ

Ephesians 2:8-9,

Ephesians 5:26,

Isaiah 53:6 & 10-12,

Matthew 10:14,

Psalms 19:7-14,

Galatians 5:22-23 (AMP),

John 4:13-14,

1 John 1:7,

John 19:33-37

Water is one of the most powerful solvents in the world. Water can slowly, over time, eat away at beach dunes. It can forcefully, with hurricane flood like waters, wash away the foundation for a road in a day. We can instantly shower away dirt. Churning water washes our clothes. We leave a pot in the sink to soak overnight to soften baked-on messes. Our bodies are mostly water, and we cannot live without it.

God knows the importance of water and uses it metaphorically throughout His Word. He knows the battles we will face, even after receiving salvation through the blood of His only Son. Accepting Jesus as our Savior, we acknowledge the blood sacrifice which gives us right standing with God. It is through His blood we are saved.

But it is the washing by the water of His Word, uttered from the living Voice, which purifies us from the things defiling us. We are saved by grace, but we are sanctified (set apart) by the washing of the water of the Word (Ephesians 2:8-9 and 5:26).

Many times we feel as though we fail in our walk with Christ because we see ourselves as lacking something. We feel pressure or anxiety because it seems God is withholding from us, so we strive or work for it *apart* from Holy Spirit, perhaps not even realizing we've gone astray (Isaiah 53:6).

God knows, even though we will one day live in Heaven, we need power to navigate the filth of the world, our old nature, and the attack of Satan and his forces. We need to learn how to "shake the dust off [our] feet" (Mark 6:11 NIV) and keep moving. That's why Romans 12 says to *renew our mind*! We cannot conform to God's way of thinking if we never find out what He's thinking!

The Bible is the water! His Word, flowing like a river in our minds, over time widens the river beds while washing away the impurities that are in us or get on us (Psalms 19:7). It cuts through the hardest of hearts. It changes the filter we see through to influence *how* we think.

Concerning the reading of his Word, read until God speaks to you. When you sense His voice, you'll know. His Word, in essence, pushes the reset button so all the fruit of the Spirit is established in a yielded heart. "But *the fruit* of the Spirit [the result of His presence within us] is love [unselfish concern for others], joy, [inner] peace, patience [not the ability to wait, but how we act while waiting], kindness, goodness, faithfulness, gentleness, self-control" (Galatians 5:22-23a AMP).

Let's not negate the importance of the living water given to us at so great a cost. The Devil has used armies to try and destroy it, legislation and media to silence it, and situations to keep us away from it. Let's devote ourselves to His Word and *be empowered with His presence* through prayer!

GRAB YOUR JOURNAL!

What is God showing you at this moment?

In light of this revelation, how does this shift your thoughts and actions?

Dream Big!

READ

Matthew 13:24-30,

Job 33:14-16,

Ephesians 3:9-21,

Acts 2:17,

Joel 2:28,

1 Corinthians 16:9,

Isaiah 42:16

Little kids have the best imagination. Sometimes they even get reality and fantasy entangled, and we have to help them know the difference, but we should encourage the right imaginations. Allow them to be superheroes and princesses. Encourage dragon slaying and feats of strength! Not only that, but if you *give* them their identity as such, they can emulate outstanding characters when you play with them. Let them help you or "rescue" you, and cheer them as the hero!

Ours is a God of imagination and dreams. He helped Abraham envision being a father of a great nation and descendants as numerous as the stars. He spoke to people in dreams. He gave wisdom to Joseph and Daniel to interpret God-given dreams. Mary daydreamed, pondering in her heart, the promise of Jesus. I wonder what she imagined His life was going to be like and how it would change hers. His Word even tells us to meditate and imagine (Acts 2:17).

Job 33:15-16 (NASB, emphasis added) says, "*In a dream*, a vision of the night, When sound sleep falls on men, *While they slumber* in their beds, Then *He opens the ears of men, And seals their instruction...*" Our imagination was created by Him. Ephesians 3:20 (NKJV) says He wants to do "*exceedingly abundantly above* all that we ask or think." I don't know about you, but I can imagine amazing things!

When God places a dream in us, it is meant to carry us through the hard places. Joseph was told the moon and stars would bow to him. But, God never told him he'd be rejected by his family, sold into slavery, lied about, and put in prison for a few years before this would take place.

Dreams and imaginings may be things we see as beyond possible or things we've yet to attain. They tend to seem far off, as we climb toward them one rung of the ladder at a time. But, dreams are there to bring hope. They are to be aspired to. Dreams keep us motivated through the tough times, training, or rejection. If we lose our ability to imagine, disappointment can grow like weeds in the garden of our heart and choke out the vision.

We can't allow what we are going through to choke out what God is planting in us. God has a way to bring us to our destiny in Him if we stay the course, listening to Holy Spirit, never jumping ahead of Him. Hardships are promised to those who walk uprightly, and it's up to us to keep our hearts free from the weeds of offenses and doubts which would keep us from our potential and our promises. God wants us to have dreams and encourage the God-given dreams of others.

Let's get in God's presence and seek His face. When we allow Him to position us for what He is dreaming, like a child, we will imagine ourselves the dragon-slayer, carrying our Sword into battle to make His dreams come to life!

GRAB YOUR JOURNAL!

What is God showing you at this moment?

In light of this revelation, how does this shift your thoughts and actions?

You're a Good Tree!

READ

Matthew 12:33-37,

John 7:27-28,

Jeremiah 17:5-8,

Colossians 1:13,

Colossians 2:6-7,

Hebrews 4:11-13,

Galatians 5:22-23,

Isaiah 16:3,

3 John 2-4,

Acts 17:28,

John 15:1-8,

Thessalonians 5:11,

1 Samuel 16:7,

James 1:2-4

We planted a Bradford Pear tree in our yard long before we built a porch on the front of the house. Now, I'm afraid it's too close. I am hoping we never have to cut it down, as I do love the shade it provides. However, we did have to cut it back a good bit on the side facing the house, so as it grows, it will hopefully branch out above the roofline. It looks a little funny now, but it's a good tree. The pruning should protect the porch we've built in case of damaging wind.

So, I'm sitting on my porch, looking at my funny-looking tree, thinking about how bad trees can't produce good fruit and good trees produce good fruit. We may see bad fruit and think we're bad because there are still areas we need to grow up in or cut off. But, if a *bad* tree *can't* produce *good* fruit, we have to rethink that notion because we have areas that *are* fruitful (Matthew 12:33-37 AMP). We have our eyes on the fruit, instead of on the tree! If we understand we have been transplanted near rivers of living water in healthy soil, soaking up nutrients, the fruit will come naturally because of its connection!!

So, what do good trees do, and how are we like them?

Trees process sunlight, converting carbon dioxide to food, and producing oxygen as a byproduct. When we spend time in God's presence (in His Light), toxic thinking, loss, pain, and circumstances that come, are swallowed up and converted through worship and intercession with thankfulness (Jeremiah 7:27-28)! Our worship becomes the byproduct that changes the air around us.

Trees receive their nourishment through their connection to the soil and produce fruit for the benefit of others. They don't eat their own fruit. We don't need to try to get love, patience, joy, etc. from other people. We become like Him, producing good fruit naturally through divine connection with Holy Spirit (Galatians 5:22-23). We then are able to bless others by giving the fruits of the Spirit away in love.

Roots are constantly growing toward a water supply, pushing deep past the drought line to get it, and have, at times, split rocks that stand in their way. In God's presence, we press in until we have received what we've purposed to believe, God's Word splitting the carnal from our spirit (Hebrews 4:11-13).

Trees are pruned to produce maximum healthy growth. They are often shaped early while their branches are young and pliable to attain the desired effect as they mature. As we yield to Holy Spirit, we take on His desire and purpose (John 15:1-8). We will be pruned, but we know that the painful process brings on maximum healthy growth.

The core of a tree allows us to determine how seasons of drought have affected an area. You can tell by its rings how much water it has received over the course of time. Wide rings are evidence of rain. Thin rings show signs of drought years. The external parts don't adequately show us what the tree has gone through. Yet, it continues to grow and provide. What people see of us only provides viewers with a glimpse into our lives, but God knows our depths (1 Samuel 16:7, 3 John 2-4).

The shade from trees protects from the heat of the day. He is the vine and we are the branches, giving shelter to those suffering from the heat, and food to those who hunger, loving and building up each other (John 3:17, 1 Thessalonians 5:11).

Trees are strengthened by resisting the wind. Through the gentle swaying, they increase in strength, so when the stronger winds come, they are less threatened. When we learn to trust Him in the little things we are strengthened for the storms that are to come (James 1:2-4).

So, let's stop focusing on producing good fruit and focus on growing up *into* Him, stay rooted in our secret place, and get the revelation that we've been planted by *Him*. In that place, the fruit will come in abundance!

GRAB YOUR JOURNAL!

What is God showing you at this moment?

In light of this revelation, how does this shift your thoughts and actions?

The Greatest Miracle

READ

Romans 8:26-30,

1 Corinthians 11:1,

Psalms 23:5,

Romans 5:6-12,

James 1:21-25 (TPT),

2 Corinthians 10:5,

Ephesians 5:1,

Philippians 4:13 (TPT),

Luke 17:20-22 (TPT),

Romans 12:1-2

If someone asked you what you're great at, would you stumble over your words, either out of humility or low self-esteem? If someone asked you what you stink at, would those words come more easily? If you answered yes, you're not alone! The world does such a great job trying to convince us of our lack of ability, talent, and resources that we can struggle to believe God can use us. Yet, we've read the Bible and have seen that those people God called all had either sin issues, weakness, or lived in obscurity.

In the modern church, many have been taught that the greatest miracle is that our "sorry selves" came to Christ and got our name in the book. Then we are to live a hopeful, yet often miserable life, waiting for the rapture and God to rescue us out of this mess and take us to Heaven. We have a "crumbs from the table" mentality, when He has prepared a table for us where our enemies can watch us dine (Psalms 23:5)!

In actuality, the greatest miracle is our transformed lives, that we are completely aware of the power of His blood, that He makes His home inside us, and *transforms* us back to *His* image, to the point where we *look like Jesus*! As we become more aware of His love for us, creating life in us, we can see others through His eyes, and love them with His love. Now that's a *powerful* miracle!

The Devil twists the world's thinking, and if we bring that thinking into our Christian walk, it pulls against us. We have to recognize this life we live is *not a mental assent to a higher standard*. It's a *transformed life*, fully submitted to *following* Christ as a disciple, not just agreeing that *He's* right and perfect, and looking to Him. It's about looking into the perfect law of liberty, casting down useless reasoning, and *becoming like Him*! In His eyes, we are prime real estate, where He intends to make His home, then establish our internal neighborhood around Him, bringing order out of chaos.

It's time we stop reasoning with a mind of the flesh that struggles against God and submit to the mind of Christ. Let's become covenant partners with Holy Spirit, so His desire becomes ours and we will accomplish all as we cooperate with Him! Let's *be* the greatest miracle as a life being transformed!

GRAB YOUR JOURNAL! | *What is God showing you at this moment?*

In light of this revelation, how does this shift your thoughts and actions?

For the Word's Sake

READ

2 Corinthians 2:14-15,

2 Corinthians 4:16-18,

Mark 4:1-30,

Matthew 14:24-27,

Matthew 16:18,

Isaiah 59:19,

James 1:2-8

I hated pop-quizzes in school! I was one who crammed at the last minute for the big test and didn't put a lot of emphasis on the quizzes along the way. I felt tricked that this mean teacher would set me up for failure! Little did I realize she wanted to know how much knowledge I was able to apply before the big test came.

Before I get into the meat of this devotion, let me say that God does not test us by setting us up for sin, bringing sickness, or hardship. Instead, He gave us His Word because He knew the times and conditions we would be living in and because we have been trained by a fallen world, twisted by darkness. He knew we needed Holy Spirit wisdom and access to supernatural power to make it through the trials and tribulations to come.

God *already knows* what is on the inside of us, so when tests come, He is not surprised. However, it does reveal to *us* the difference in what we say we believe and what has become *rooted truth* in us. In Mark 4, the parable of the seed and the sower, Jesus says persecution comes for the *Word's sake*. If our heart ground is hard, we will excuse the seed of His Word as not applicable to us, and it will be instantly stolen. When we are all hungry for the good things God can do for us—having our needs met, salvation, a miracle or two thrown in, we receive His Word gladly. But, when the weeds of pressures and troubles come, the promises get squeezed out, and we find ourselves wondering where God is, putting His love on trial, proving we are in this life for the gift at the expense of the Giver, rather than our lives delivered from darkness and a transformed heart.

Storms come because the Devil hates God. He knows he can't destroy God but wants to destroy Him inside of us, setting himself on the throne of our hearts. It is *only* when we are rooted and grounded *in God's love*, and the storm comes, we find we can weather its abuse. Then, those in the world can see we are not at the mercy of the *same* storm and afflictions they are. When we are pressed, the fragrance of Christ is diffused out of us. The amount of peace *that is a part of us* will sometimes surprise us because of His Word that rises up in us like a fortified wall against the flood!

We *can* count it all joy when we fall into trials and testing, knowing we have *an* Advocate, a covenant, and a testimony in the making, and "We view our slight, short-lived troubles in the light of eternity. We see our difficulties as the substance that produces for us an *eternal*, weighty glory far beyond all comparison..." (2 Corinthians 4:17 TPT) while we keep our eyes on eternal things.

GRAB YOUR JOURNAL! | *What is God showing you at this moment?*
In light of this revelation, how does this shift your thoughts and actions?

Where Y'all From?

READ
John 3:1-21,
John 16:17,
Ephesians 2:6-7,
Ephesians 5:1-2,
1 Peter 2:10-12,
Acts 17:28,
Ephesians 4:13-15

When I went to my daughter's Marine Corps Intel school graduation, I met a young Marine from New York, who had never experienced a real-life southern accent. He was so enamored by it, he asked my daughter in his thick New York Italian accent if he could hear her mom "talk again." If you've ever heard my voice, you'd know what a love child of Dolly Parton and Larry the Cable Guy would sound like.

My hometown of Fayetteville, NC is a melting pot of various cultures, nationalities, and just different parts of the country. We get to enjoy diverse cultures and dialects, and we've learned how to tell where people are from. At the very least, we can tell "they ain't from here."

We inherit certain traits from our parents and others from where we were raised. Our looks come from our parents; our style comes from our surroundings; our tolerance for temperature and our accents comes from our region. Aspects of our temperament may be inherited, but the way we typically respond to circumstances is learned—good or bad—through example.

Once we are *born into* the kingdom of God, we begin to take on an entirely new language, tolerance, and response to circumstances. We pick up the traits of our *Father*, and steward those attributes as we learn Kingdom culture. As we become more like Jesus, people may not distinguish where we're from, but they soon realize that we "ain't from 'round here" (John 17:16).

In John 3, a Pharisee named Nicodemus came to see Jesus. Nicodemus said the Pharisees believed the miracles Jesus did came from God but stumbled over the idea of being born again. Jesus pointed out if Nicodemus couldn't understand natural things which paralleled the spirit realm, how would he receive spiritual revelation? Some revelations are born of flesh through reasoning, training, or knowledge. But, others are born of the Spirit through revelation, transformation, and sanctification.

If we're experiencing frustration from reading scripture or listening to a sermon, we may be missing out on spirit-breathed revelation. We're trying to filter a heavenly message through an earthly perspective. Without the Spirit, without the foundation of the love of Christ, we run the risk of seeming mean and religious, or victimized by our emotions, trying to live up to some man-made doctrine we don't believe in our hearts.

Divine revelation comes from Holy Spirit to us and through us. No one else may know where it's coming from or be able to see where it's going, but they'll sense it just like the wind (John 3:8). Jesus left His home in Heaven (John 3:13) to make heavenly realms available to us through Holy Spirit when we are born again (Ephesians 2:6-7).

We develop His "*accent*," His temperament, His way of handling injustices, by *spending time* with Him. Ephesians 5:1 says we are to imitate Him; but we can't *truly* know Christ by hearing *about* Him, no more than we can *know* someone by looking at their photo albums. We might get an idea of them, but until we spend time together, our revelation is limited. As we come into the unity of faith, we will change from the inside out. Some changes may be instant. Others will be gradual. But people who witness our lives will either glorify God, or at the very least, recognize that we are not from around here.

GRAB YOUR JOURNAL!

What is God showing you at this moment?

In light of this revelation, how does this shift your thoughts and actions?

Don't Go Back!

READ

Numbers 13,

Deuteronomy 30:15-20,

John 10:11-17,

Jeremiah 17:5-8, 2

Corinthians 10:2-5,

2 Corinthians 3:17-18,

Proverbs 3:5-6,

Romans 8:14-19,

Psalms 16:11,

Acts 2:28

When Moses sent the twelve spies into Jericho to check out the land God had promised the Israel-ites, only two of them (Joshua and Caleb) came back with any positive feedback. Everyone else said, "It's true that the land has everything God said it had, but those people are giants. We looked like grasshoppers compared to them. We're sure they thought so too" (Numbers 13:32-33, my paraphrase)!

Some of the Israelites had already tried to con-vince God's people to turn back when the going got tough in the wilderness. They reasoned that Pharaoh's army had just died in the Red Sea. The country was in ruins from the plagues. Maybe they could negotiate a deal.

God had given the promise, but He left out all those pesky little details about giants. He already knew about the giants and wasn't *threatened* by them. Had He said, "Hey, if y'all will just walk around the city wall a few times, I'll col-lapse it and give y'all the city," maybe they wouldn't have balked at Joshua and Caleb. But, God wanted them to trust Him and learn a little bit about obedience and blessings rather than appearance and circumstance.

Their decision based on doubt and fear delayed everyone, along with Joshua and Caleb, from their destiny for forty years! It bound them and their families to wander through the desert. Even though they were fully provided for with manna, clothes that wouldn't wear out, and God's own heating and cooling system, they were merely existing and surviving. Everyone over twenty would die in the wilderness having never fulfilled their destiny.

Similar to the Israelites, there will be people who try to convince us to go back where we came from because they haven't been where we've been, or know what we've been through. They *cannot* be in our shoes, and have no idea what it took to set us free. There are circumstances that were painful, but familiar, which cry out for us to return, so at least we don't have to fear the unknown giants.

There is nothing in our past worth going back for! No one has the investment in our future that we do. We cross paths with some and journey with others *for a time*, but no one or no *thing* has earned the right to be the Director of our destiny but *God*! They have nothing to lose if we fail to reach our destiny, and they will jump into someone else's journey if ours doesn't fit in their comfort zones!

We all face situations where we have to make the choice whether or not we are going to trust in God or ourselves. Deuteronomy 30:19 (AMP) says, "I call heaven and earth as witnesses against you today, that I have set before you life and death, the blessing and the curse; therefore, you shall choose life in order that you may live, you and your descendants…"

There's more on the line than we know. Someone is counting on our determination to trust God when everything around us is telling us it's not worth it.

God gives us a choice. In that choice lies another choice, and another, from glory to glory, from each valley to mountaintop, bringing us closer to fully relying on Him, until we fulfill our destiny. Let's not bend to the whisperers and doubters who are on our journey with us, who want us to remain with them so they can stay comfortable. Let's focus on His purpose for our lives, like obedient children, from the path of slavery to the Promised Land!

GRAB YOUR JOURNAL!

What is God showing you at this moment?

In light of this revelation, how does this shift your thoughts and actions?

Encouraging Yourself in the Lord!

READ

Psalm 84:6-7,

John 7:38,

Hebrews 11:1 & 6,

Philippians 4:6-9,

Ephesians 3:13-20,

Psalms 19:6-14,

1 Timothy 6:12,

Zephaniah 3:16-17,

Isaiah 26:3,

Psalms 24:4-10,

Ephesians 6:10-12,

Micah 7:8,

Proverbs 24:16,

Joshua 1:9

Have you ever seen cheerleaders on the sidelines booing their team when they were down 50-0? It doesn't happen. They wear their uniforms. They support their team's efforts. They have practiced a script from which they do not veer. Even when the fans, whose faces and body language have long since given up hope of a win, are stunned into silence, the cheerleaders keep cheering. The crowd may dwindle as they leave to escape the beat down, but those who wear their team's colors continue to encourage each other.

It's easy to cheer when your team is winning, but it takes a lot of strength to rally the troops, keep the faith, and encourage those around you when loss looks imminent. When we are a part of a team or a plan, we don't give up on it. We know our team's resolve. We've watched them practice. We know the integrity of the coach. We believe there is something inside that will eventually prevail. More importantly, the coach is instilling a lot more into his team than can ever be found on a scoreboard.

As Christians, we're on God's side. There may be times when it looks like we're losing. We may have even lost a battle. But, the *season* is not over. We continue to cheer, praising and worshiping Him, and encouraging ourselves! It's not hypocrisy to thank God when we don't see a way out. 1 Samuel 30:6 says when David was greatly distressed, he encouraged himself in the Lord his God. In the midst of great loss, when his own men wanted to stone him, he was able to get still, center himself, and inquire of the Lord as to what he should do.

Psalms 84:5-7 (AMP, emphasis added) says, "Blessed *and greatly favored* is the man whose strength is in You, In whose heart are the highways to Zion. Passing through the Valley of Weeping (Baca), they make it a place of springs; The early rain also covers it with blessings. They go from strength to strength [increasing in victorious power]..."

Because their hearts are the actual roads leading to God, their tears turn a place of weeping into life-giving springs! When we treat our hearts as roads by which the presence of God travels, it's easier to encourage ourselves and establish ourselves in faith.

When we question the goodness of God and His love for us in the midst of the battles of our lives, we set up roadblocks. We may say we have faith because we can regurgitate what we've been taught, but it isn't faith if we're excusing ourselves or accusing God. Faith isn't mature until the epic battle to believe is *superseded* by the *peace* that *goes beyond* our understanding and quiets our souls. The Devil's job is simple, and he has had years to perfect it; to rattle us to the point where God is unseated from the throne of our hearts. There are times when we are going to have to encourage ourselves in the Lord, to be our own cheerleaders, knowing our Coach has the strategy for ultimate success. We may lose a battle here and there, but the end game is already won! Be strong and take courage!

GRAB YOUR JOURNAL!

What is God showing you at this moment?

In light of this revelation, how does this shift your thoughts and actions?

End the Debate

READ

Matthew 11:4-10,

Matthew 16:13-20,

Matthew 24:4,

1 Corinthians 9:26-27,

Hebrews 12:1-2, 2

Corinthians 10:3-6,

Hebrews 10:23,

Galatians 5:17,

1 Peter 5:8,

Ephesians 6:10-18

Jesus asked His disciples, "Who do men say I am?" They gave Him a variety of answers. Then He asked, "Who do *YOU* say I am?" and revelation came out of Peter's mouth. "You are the Anointed One, the Son of the living God" (Matthew 16:16 TPT, emphasis added)!

In Matthew 11, when John the Baptist was in prison, awaiting beheading, he sent his disciples to Jesus, whom he had prophesied about and baptized, asking, "Are You the One, or should we look for another?" After all, John was a prophet. He had believed Jesus would be the deliverer Moses was, leading His people out of captivity and into glory! But, his present predicament looked as if he had made a terrible error. His circumstances were so big his faith was put to the test. Jesus sent word to John about all the miracles and to tell him "... that the blessing of heaven comes upon those who never lose their faith in me—no matter what happens" (Matthew 11:6 TPT)! Then, He honored John as a prophet to the crowd.

There are times when we struggle to believe truth; when lies seem easier and sound way more comfortable. An *obvious solution presents itself* but can be so deceptive. Proverbs 4:23 (TPT) says to "... guard the affections of your heart, for they affect all that you are." Matthew 24:4 (NASB) says, "... See to it that no one misleads you."

If we must guard our hearts, and not be misled, there inevitably will be facts, thoughts, and ways which seem to be easier and better which will attempt to pull us away from the truth of God's word.

This is why God speaks of *endurance, training, casting down*, and *clinging* to

Him! We cannot be led by vain imaginations, fear, or crafty words which cause us to debate what God has already established as *truth*. Our primary goal in this life is to know Jesus and His love for us. We owe no man anything but love. We're not to war against flesh and blood or struggle against Holy Spirit, but rather submit to truth, then seek the Comforter in our *uncomfortable*.

Let's draw a line in the sand when it comes to the chatter of the world or our present circumstances. There is no need to rehash useless arguments or look for another way out. For the Christian, the debate is over. So having done all, *we stand firm*.

GRAB YOUR JOURNAL!

What is God showing you at this moment?

In light of this revelation, how does this shift your thoughts and actions?

Then, All of a Sudden!

READ

Mark 4:21-34,

Romans 8:1-11,

Hebrews 5:13-14,

Matthew 18:2-4

As a teacher assistant, I would occasionally drive a bus for someone who was absent. One Friday, there was a tiny little kindergartener on the bus who had quite a few behavioral issues. She was famous for her wild antics. But since she was only on the bus for about five minutes, I thought, No big deal. *Was I wrong*! From the moment she got on, this little stick of dynamite was out of control. As her stop approached, she climbed under the seat and would not come out. With mom waiting outside the bus, seemingly unaffected by the scene, I got up, pulled her out from under the seat, while her legs were wrapped around the seat leg. Once I got her to the aisle, she planted all fours against the seats in front of her tiny, yet strong frame. If it had been in a movie, my feverish wrestling with this relentless five-year-old to hand her off to mom would have been hilarious!

As I drove away frustrated, trying to regain composure, I heard Holy Spirit chuckle, "Not quite as dead in the area of impatience as you thought, huh?" It had been a while since I had experienced an outburst like that, and God was using it as a teachable moment. In this situation, I was agitated and impatient, which *surely* didn't manifest Christ's nature to anyone around me.

In Mark 4:17, persecution springs up to choke out the Word of God. It shows us how much of Him is in us and to what degree we've become Christlike. We find out how deep the roots go when those sudden storms come to rip out our neatly planted gardens!

It's those *suddenlies* which seem to slam us off track. In the natural, we can never be prepared. But, we don't have to stay derailed by our natural mindset. We cannot afford to allow how we've reacted to bring condemnation. Rather, a quick reflection to our current position can realign us to the path God has intended. The moment of reflection is simply to allow us to see *we still have a place to go* in Christ; this mere knowledge of what we've read and heard shows us what we must *learn by practice and experience.*

There is *no condemnation in Christ*! We keep a childlike heart, meaning, we are always correctable, always curious, always learning, and always dependent. I wasn't prepared for the little storm that day, but I'm leaning in to hear Papa's wisdom. I know *I'm* not the *fixer* of every child, but now I see where I need to partner with Holy Spirit, so I will be more discerning, putting what He is showing me into practice for the next *suddenly.*

GRAB YOUR JOURNAL!

What is God showing you at this moment?

In light of this revelation, how does this shift your thoughts and actions?

Dealing With Failed Expectations

READ

Ephesians 4:21-32,

1 Corinthians 13,

Romans 5:8,

John 10:10,

John 15:12-13,

John 14:6,

Ephesians 5:1-2,

Hebrews 10:19-26,

Colossians 3,

Psalms 34:8-14,

1 John 4:7-8,

2 Peter 1:3

In my younger days, speed limits seemed like merely suggestions. Stop lights were a personal affront to me. I wasn't simply driving to work, I was *racing*. It was all fun and games, but since then, I've mellowed out in my need for speed. I have no problem moving out of the way for my fellow racers, praying they and those whose bumpers they ride, get where they're going safely.

It's the road-rager who concerns me; always in a hurry and cursing those who aren't. By the time they arrive at their destination, their tone is set for the day. Never mind they didn't leave on time or make time for delays. I can only estimate they were already angry. But, fellow drivers take the brunt, and traffic takes the blame, and they can deny responsibility for their anger, impatience, and behavior toward others.

Sadly, some of us have the same attitude in other areas of life. While our kids are developing, we may expect perfection in things they are just learning, becoming impatient when we have to tell them things more than a few times. We might get frustrated when coworkers don't put the emphasis on our requests because ours are the most urgent—to us. When someone forgets an important event, we may use their failure to manipulate them. If we're not careful, we allow our impatience to turn to anger with each missed assumption.

There are times we will experience disappointment when others fail to meet our expectations. But when it affects us so deeply that we close ourselves off or quit believing for the sake of others (1 Corinthians 13:7), we are not walking in the love to which God has called us. We've all disappointed someone and been judged according to a moment of weakness. Yet God, in His mercy, still loves us, calls us righteous, and continues to beckon us into the life we were meant for. It's only when we take for granted Holy Spirit's influence that we grieve Him (Ephesians 4:30 TPT). He calls us to be like Him. He didn't just say, "Love Me," He said, "Follow Me in the life I modeled for you" (John 14:6). If it were not possible, He wouldn't have commanded it (John 15:12).

If we are experiencing lack, it's possible we don't *know* Him intimately in an area (1 John 4:7-8). When we pray, we should ask to be shown His strength in that place: "God, show me who You are in this. Help me to know You in this area of my weakness." Whether it's time management, relationships, parenting, finances, intimacy with a spouse, work ethic, food choices, a mind in turmoil, He is the answer! Everything pertaining to life and godliness is found in Jesus (2 Peter 1:3), and we are empowered when we receive Holy Spirit and ask Him to guide us.

Learning takes time, and obedience is intentional and deliberate. Sometimes it may feel forced or uncomfortable. But, this is when we know we're moving by faith instead of feelings. Let's take the time to be intimately acquainted with Him in *every* aspect, learning to imitate Him in every circumstance, with a heart fully committed to holding fast until we see ourselves looking like Him!

GRAB YOUR JOURNAL!

What is God showing you at this moment?

In light of this revelation, how does this shift your thoughts and actions?

Your Eyes Are in Front of Your Head

READ

Ephesians 4:13-15,

James 3:15-17,

James 1:2-27,

Matthew 5:14-16,

1 John 4:7-8,

2 Corinthians 5:19-20

Have you ever noticed the difference between animals of prey and predators? It's in the eyes. Some animals of prey have eyes on the sides of their heads so they can see what might be sneaking up behind them. They have a wide peripheral. They are always on the defensive and sensitive to their surroundings, ready to take flight at any moment. When one member of the herd flees, they all flee. Their daily reality is to survive.

In comparison, the eyes of most predators are forward-facing, made for the hunt. Lions, for instance, are always on the offensive. They don't need to worry about their surroundings. If one is attacked, others will come to their defense. As king of the jungle, they rule their territories with confidence and without fear. They wake up ready for the hunt.

When God created man in His own image, He put man's eyes on the front of his head and gave him authority over all of creation (Genesis 1:26). After sin twisted what God had created, man began to live outside of his created value. Before the fall, he was naked and *unashamed*, but after he sinned, he became *self-aware*, trying to hide from God (Genesis 3:8-10). What was once love became selfishness, birthed out of fear, and it has been perpetuated in humanity ever since.

We lost our identity as children of God and became like the prey animals, living in fear of our surroundings, intimidated by every social, political, and cultural condition, at the mercy of the Devil and this world's system.

We left *intercession* to become activists, bashing, protesting, and kicking up our heels at every perceived injustice, proving fear drives every move. We live in response to the headline of the day, hoping we won't be *swallowed up* by evil (James 3:15-17). Sometimes, we do nothing to allow God to shine through us nor to expose the darkness that has captured the world (Matthew 5:14-16). When this happens consistently, it reveals we need to get to know God *more* (1 John 4:7-8).

God sent Jesus to model what we are supposed to look like and gave us Holy Spirit to recreate a sinless, condemnation-free, holy, born-again image in us, restoring us to what we were before sin entered the picture. Jesus focused His eyes forward, undaunted by those who were convicted by His life. Now, God has strategically placed us in this day, this time, and in this community to take authority over the enemy (which is Satan, not people). We are here to dispel darkness, *not add to the confusion*. Where we are is where we have been assigned. If God puts a desire in us to see change, let's start with our own sphere of influence. Let's get in God's presence and pray for wisdom for ourselves, government and spiritual leaders, police officers, and protesters.

Let's see ourselves as ambassadors of God and ministers of reconciliation (2 Corinthians 5:19-20) on a love assignment from Heaven, bringing hope, light, and truth to the territory we are assigned!

GRAB YOUR JOURNAL!

What is God showing you at this moment?

In light of this revelation, how does this shift your thoughts and actions?

Releasing Forgiveness

READ

Matthew 18:12-35,

Colossians 1:13-14,

Micah 7:18-19,

Matthew 5:43-48,

Matthew 6:15

A friend of mine and of many in the community, was brutally murdered. Mike Mansfield was a big, gruff, bear of a guy whom God delivered out of a life of drug addiction. His response to God was turning his mess into his mission; to love and bring Christ to a rough area of town. He helped the homeless and ex-convicts, serving meals and holding church services at his carwash. As he stood in front of our Savior and heard the words, "Well done," I can almost hear him argue, "But I wasn't finished yet!"

A flood of emotion struck me when I heard the news; disbelief, sadness, and anger at his killers and even despair at what might become of his employees and the homeless and downtrodden he ministered to on a weekly basis. Immediately, I heard God say, "You know—Mike forgives them."

Forgiveness can be tough when we don't fully understand what it does for us. Not only does forgiveness release us from the toxicity of emotionally driven responses, but it literally brings healing to the joints and heart. It's also a spiritual force we release which allows Holy Spirit to work in a situation to manifest Himself in a greater way. Jesus asked His Father to forgive us because we didn't know what we were doing when we crucified Him.

God was so adamant about forgiveness, He sent Jesus to pay the price to reconcile us to Him while we were not only in the midst of our sin but enjoying it! In Matthew 18, Jesus teaches a parable regarding the gravity of unforgiveness, saying if we don't forgive, God will hold us accountable for our debts.

When I taught children's church, I used the illustration of a door in the classroom to show how forgiveness works. I would have a child go outside the door and try to get in while others would hold it shut. The door represented the entry point to our heart. If the door was closed, forgiveness couldn't go out, but neither could it come in.

We are called to forgive when it's inconvenient. We forgive sacrificially, when we don't want to. We forgive because we have been forgiven. We forgive because we believe the offender would never have done what they did if they had known who they are in Christ. Our greatest revenge on darkness would be to snatch the offender from Satan's grip and create another hell-crusher for Christ.

If we choose not to forgive, how are we any different than the world (Matthew 5:43-48)? If we choose to stay offended, we stand in opposition of Christ's blood which brings healing.

Let's not allow the enemy to dominate our hearts nor lose one inch of ground that believers like Mike, who have gone before us have taken. Let's pray for those who persecute us. Pray, lest we fall into the snare of the enemy. When we infuse the love of Christ into our situation and choose God's way over our own, we will be surprised at the strength He brings to overcome.

GRAB YOUR JOURNAL! | *What is God showing you at this moment?*
In light of this revelation, how does this shift your thoughts and actions?

New Wine in Old Wine Skins

READ

Matthew 9:17,

Mark 2:22,

Romans 12:1-2,

Ephesians 5:1-2,

1 John 4:7-20,

Philippians 2:12,

Hebrews 11:6, 2

Corinthians 5:17-21

Have you ever known someone whose life seems like a result of many bad decisions; maybe someone who had been successful in high school whose life has fallen apart? We wonder *how* they managed to fall so far. We may have heard stories of very poor people who won the lottery only to lose every penny. More than likely, they either didn't have a support network or didn't have the tools to make things work.

We are conditioned to think the government or some agency should be able to fix these problems. We may think it should be easy to fix. All they need is a job or a home. And they do! But, *without a new mindset*, many will fall back into the old habits which perpetuated their downward spiral.

Jesus told His disciples in Mark 2:22a (AMP), "No one puts new wine into old wine skins." Typically, goat skin was used to make bottles for wine. As the new wine went in and fermented, it bubbled and expanded, working its way into the new soft skin. It absorbed the liquid, allowing it to move and expand throughout the fermentation process. When it was finished, the skin would become hard like a bottle, so if new wine was poured in again, it couldn't flex and would burst under the pressure.

When we are born again, we are like new wine skin. As the *new wine* of the gospel is poured in, it begins to work its way into the fabric of our being. We allow it to change our thinking and shape us from the inside out. Our decision making *process* changes. When our heart's cry is to please Him out of a grateful heart, deepening relationship and revelation, we *do* out of an unselfish nature which is being worked into us. If we become tough and inflexible old wineskins, we will not be able to absorb and contain Holy Spirit, we will be broken, and He will be lost on us.

It is essential to be transformed by renewing our minds, constantly conforming to His image of love. It's easier to work out what has been worked in than to conform to a set of rules out of obligation. Let's get rid of any self-defeating thoughts, attitudes, and habits that have produced hardness in areas we haven't fully submitted to the new wine of Holy Spirit, taking shape inside of us, so we resemble Christ's image!

GRAB YOUR JOURNAL!

What is God showing you at this moment?

In light of this revelation, how does this shift your thoughts and actions?

Let the First Thing Be the First Thing

READ

Proverbs 3:5-10,

Proverbs 4:4-13,

Hebrews 12:1-7,

Romans 10:17,

Proverbs 16:9,

1 John 2:20,

Matthew 6:33,

1 Corinthians 3:2-4

My husband is pretty health conscious. He has a mentally and physically demanding job but still manages to get his workout in on his lunch hour most days. It has definitely helped with the aches and pains associated with age and joint stress of working at UPS for over thirty-six years. One day, he tweaked a back muscle, so he made an adjustment to how he would step off his truck. After a bit, he took some pain meds. That evening, as he soaked in a hot bath and epsom salt, he heard Holy Spirit say, "You act like an atheist." Knowing better than to argue with God, and knowing God needed to say something to provoke his spirit and get his attention, he waited for Him to continue. "Not once did it even enter your mind to ask Me to heal you." Upon hearing this, conviction came. He repented and worshiped His loving Father in the tub, thanking Him for the revelation and correction.

We are made up of spirit, soul, and body. We are spirit, living in a body, and our soul is a combination of our mind, will, and emotions. Once we are born again, our spirits are made perfect toward God. However, our minds are in constant need of renewal. Many times, as in my husband's case, our minds get so overwhelmed by all we've got to do, we let the Word slip. It is not always the *first* thing.

None of the things my husband did on that day were wrong, except for the fact that none of them included Holy Spirit.

There are things we must train ourselves to do by reason of practice to sharpen our spiritual senses (Hebrews 5:14). We can even be so sharp in one area that we totally miss another, and the Devil is always seeking to find places we've allowed to become a soft target.

It's not enough to go to church and practice good works. It takes filling our eyes, ears, mouths, and hearts with His Word, looking at everyone and everything through our Father's eyes, and taking time to hear His voice above the noise of "the way of natural man" (1 Corinthians 3:3, my paraphrase).

That's why *daily* and oftentimes minute-to-minute communication with Holy Spirit should be the higher wisdom we seek, the voice we must hear, and the anointing we intentionally follow. We need to consciously make *Him the first thing* until He's so embedded in our subconscious that He becomes *our* first thing (Proverbs 16:9)!

Let's open His Word and ask Him to show us *all* things by revealing truth to our hearts and *become* what we read. Let's worship God as He convicts, corrects, and changes us from glory to glory, learning to *see Him first in everything*!

GRAB YOUR JOURNAL!

What is God showing you at this moment?

In light of this revelation, how does this shift your thoughts and actions?

The Power of Grace

READ

Hebrews 6:1-4,

Matthew 10:8,

Galatians 3:15-29,

Matthew 5:21-48,

Romans 6:1-20,

Galatians 5:22-23

In my opinion, Christianity 101 is this: Heal the sick, raise the dead, cleanse lepers, cast out devils, freely give and receive, based on Jesus' words in Matthew 10:8. We know we need Jesus for these things. After all, He's the One who provides the miracle. We are simply to move in obedience, right? But, what I'm coming to realize is I need Him for much more than just what I consider "the big things."

In Hebrews 6:1, the author tells believers they should move on to spiritual maturity, without having to reteach basic principles like salvation, repentance from dead works, healing, and raising the dead. Personally, I would never have thought of raising the dead as basic.

The truth is, we can do *nothing* without Holy Spirit. Releasing our hearts by forgiving someone who has hurt us or our family, loving someone who is entirely unlovable, humility in unfair treatment, and patience for *anything*, are all impossible without *His empowering grace*.

When we become followers of Christ, we are lifted out of one kingdom and placed into another. We move from the law of death, written on stone, to the law of grace, written in the heart (Hebrews 8:10). The law shows us we will always come up short, and as long as we struggle under it, we'll be sorely disappointed. Under grace, everything we do now is to be an outward expression of what God is working into us. Grace is God's divine influence, unmerited favor, and empowerment in the heart to do what the law demanded. However, grace actually has a stiffer requirement.

John 1:17 says the law was given by Moses, but Grace and truth came through Jesus. The law says don't commit adultery. However, Jesus (Grace & Truth) taught you've already committed adultery if you've lusted in your heart. The law also says don't murder. But again, Grace (Jesus) taught if you are angry with another or are calling someone harsh names, you are in danger of a similar judgement as a murderer would get. In other words, turning the other cheek and going the extra mile shows a lot more maturity than the law's "eye for an eye" or giving only what is deserved. God is looking at our hearts not merely our actions. It is impossible to live this way without God's empowering grace, which only comes through practicing daily surrender, having our senses sharpened, as we become transformed into love.

The *fruit* (the evidence) of the Spirit is "love, joy, peace, patience, kindness, goodness, faithfulness, gentleness, and self-control" (Galatians 5:22-23a ESV). The fruit is planted (revealed) in seed form, then, must be *cultivated*. We don't get frustrated at a seed in the ground for not producing. We tend to it, giving it what it needs to grow, knowing it will eventually produce a harvest.

Grace is *empowered* by *love*. God is *Love*. The more time we spend with Him, the more He's going to rub off on our hearts. In tending to the ground, we find fruit appearing without forcing it. It becomes part of who we are as we become one with Him. Those things which once provoked and hurt us suddenly no longer have a say in our lives. When we are empowered by grace, sin against us doesn't produce sin in us.

Instead of being at the mercy of our emotions, let's receive mercy from the throne of Grace to give us peace in the midst of every storm. Let's go in grace!

GRAB YOUR JOURNAL! | *What is God showing you at this moment?*

In light of this revelation, how does this shift your thoughts and actions?

Captain America: Civil War

READ

Matthew 6:22-23,

James 3:11-13,

Matthew 5:13-16,

Isaiah 50:4-11,

Jeremiah 17:8,

Romans 14:17,

1 Corinthians 3:1-3 (AMP),

2 Corinthians 5:21,

John 14:27,

Psalms 28:7

My family and I were enjoying one of the Avenger movies, *Captain America: Civil War*, where the villain, overtaken by grief, blamed the Avengers for the loss of his family in the city where the superheroes had fought a fierce battle. He sought to retaliate against them, but realizing he couldn't physically destroy the superheroes, he found a way to divide them, causing them to destroy each other.

By exploiting their pasts, preying on their guilt and regrets, and emphasizing their different ideologies, he created a *spirit of division* which spawned an all-out war in what had been a functioning (albeit dysfunctional) family. *The world was left helpless while those who were tasked to save it fought each other.*

As the body of Christ, we cannot afford to allow the appetites of the world to take our eyes off Jesus. Satan is a master of division and distraction. His heart is full of vengeance from his fall from Heaven, but he knows he cannot knock God off his throne. He also knows our born-again spirit is untouchable. However, he has found ways to render us ineffective, prolonging his demise.

The Devil works very hard to distract us by stirring up physical desires, whether it be personal gratification, selfishness, fear, revenge, or our differences to snare us. As our emotions tear at us, he twists our intellect to *justify our feelings* until our *actions* are in his power. Once he has obtained a foothold, it is only a matter of time before we implode.

Matthew 6:22-23 says that the eye is the lamp of the body and if our eye is in God's light, then we are *full of light*. But if we're focused on other things, our eyes are darkened and our body is *filled with great darkness*.

Things we have struggled to forget, kept hidden, walked away from, or built walls to protect from further damage can eat away at us like cancer. Faith in His love allows Holy Spirit to reveal and destroy those ideologies or habits we created which have become a ball and chain to us.

Let's not be afraid to confront and drive out shame that isolates us, fear, or weakness in our flesh which keeps us tied to our past. We've been given the keys to the Kingdom, with access to *everything* that produces life and godliness with Kingdom power! We've been made righteous (2 Corinthians 5:21), *given peace* (John 14:27), *strengthened* by joy (Psalms 28:7).

Let's be *so* determined to walk in the freedom purchased by Christ's blood that strongholds fall from our lives, and His love keeps us firmly rooted, *controlled* by righteousness, peace, and joy in our own lives and as a unified body of Christ!

GRAB YOUR JOURNAL!

What is God showing you at this moment?

In light of this revelation, how does this shift your thoughts and actions?

Sympathy vs. Compassion

READ

Matthew 5:40-46,

Hebrews 10:20-25,

Hebrews 4:15,

James 2:14-26,

Philippians 2:12-13,

Hebrews 11:1-3

A couple of years ago, I was praying over a certain situation. At that point, I had been praying for several years, and the more I prayed, it seemed the worse things became! I was struggling with my faith because I couldn't see *how* God could bring about a change when things seemed to be getting worse. I relayed my frustration to my best friend, who stopped me in my tracks. "You *know* what God's Word says! You *know* what He has promised! It doesn't matter what it *looks* like…" Wow! A word in season!

It took a couple more years of interceding, but I did so with a different mindset—and the promise has begun to be fulfilled!

I thank God for friends who provoke me in faith—friends who stir me to good works—and won't allow me to remain the same! While I know there are times we feel like we need to share our hearts, our hurts, our faults, it should never be with the intent to rally people to our side. It should be with the full intent of challenging the oppressive spirit that is holding our head to the ground!

We need to be very careful with whom we share our troubles or weaknesses. Not all counsel is Christ-centered, even if it may be coming from a Christian. We might find someone who will lick our wounds and give us reasons why we can't manifest Christ in the midst of a situation. We need to be aligned to Holy Spirit, so we know when we're hearing a comfortable lie from a sympathetic person that would cause us to remain in familiar pain because our battle is uncomfortable.

It is okay to cry with people and to be touched by the feeling of their infirmity, but if in our compassion, we don't call them to their identity in Christ, we have done them an injustice. I think leaving the healing, restorative power of God out of a situation makes us either like the world or a "form of religion" without power!

Jesus was caring and compassionate, and His love for people caused Him to challenge the religious oppression of the Pharisee (Matthew 23:33), the offense in Martha (Luke 10:41-42), and the demonic influence of his disciples (Matthew 16:23). God will always go after what is standing *in the way* of love without focusing on the sin. But, God places much more value on the state of our hearts than our comfort level.

Faith without works is dead. But, works without faith is simply *ideology*. Everything we do should be with the revelation that God is *in us*, working out of us what He is working into us (Phillipians 2:12-13)! If we are going to be free from the effects of the fire, we have to be able to dance in the heat. If we are going to get through the storm, we are going to have to be able to sleep in the back of the boat! For it is by faith that the worlds are formed and created (Hebrews 11:3)! So, what are we creating in ours?

GRAB YOUR JOURNAL!

What is God showing you at this moment?

In light of this revelation, how does this shift your thoughts and actions?

Hurt Because of You Or Hurting For You?

READ

Philippians 2:1-3 (NET),

1 Corinthians 13:1-10 (MSG),

Romans 12 (TPT)

I had the opportunity to get my feelings hurt this week. But, I didn't take it. Sometimes insecurity stemming from our past can raise its ugly head and sink our spiritual boat with useless thinking: *What have I done wrong NOW? Have I missed something somewhere?* What we regard as a problem between us and someone else might just be their internal battle, and we just happen to be on the receiving end. We may serve as reminders of some weakness, contention, or anxiety they are dealing with, and our very presence can be an irritation.

Thoughts deeply rooted in feelings need to be inspected for lies and weeded regularly. We cannot just allow our feelings to rule our thinking. When those hurt feelings flared up, Holy Spirit allowed me to go down the proverbial rabbit hole of feeling sorry for myself and insecure for about ten minutes before putting the brakes on; long enough for me to become aware of the wall I was building around my thought-life. I'll share His words to me as seed sown:

"When are you going to pray about what's bothering this person, instead of how it's affecting you? Is that the way I love *you*? This person is hurting, and you've *made this about you*. Let's turn this around.

Some things are not yours to know. What others think of you is not your business. *I* am your business, and *you are Mine*. The same way boats get stuck on the shore as the tide goes out, you've allowed yourself to get stuck in the shallows when I've called you into the deep. Shallow thoughts will make you run ashore and become dry-docked. There's no faith in criticizing.

Are you walking in love? Are your thoughts for their good? Why not see the struggle of their heart instead of the selfish desire to be seen as worthy and good in their eyes?

The way *you're* perceiving their thoughts and feelings toward you, *good or bad*, is not only fruitless but *idolatry*.

Love is patient, kind, doesn't keep a record of wrongs, doesn't force itself on others—*this* is the kind of *love* I have called you to *be*. It doesn't falter. It can't be hurt. It's untouchable because I live in you! Stop giving place to the Devil."

As much as it depends on us, we must walk in harmony with those in our sphere of influence. If we're unaware we may have offended a person, ask with an open and humble heart—not ready to defend ourselves but to open dialogue. If they refuse, then the fight is not ours, and they need our prayers.

Let's start *seeing truth* and *becoming love*. Let's *defend* the spiritually weak. Let's take up arms against the *real enemy* who is stealing from the hearts and lives of the children God loves.

GRAB YOUR JOURNAL!

What is God showing you at this moment?

In light of this revelation, how does this shift your thoughts and actions?

Loving Hell Out of People

READ

1 Corinthians 13:4-7
(MSG),

1 John 4:18,

1 Peter 5:5-9 (AMP),

John 13:34-35,

Ephesians 4:13-32 (AMP),

Philippians 2:12

I know that title may offend some, but it's what I woke up with in my spirit. Love hell out of people, and *love* them into Christ!

Most everyone knows about the "Love Chapter" in 1 Corinthians 13, but I often wonder if we fully get it! When we read it, maybe we think, *God is Love, so this describes Him*, or we might believe if we were to love like this, we would be doormats for someone to step on. Well, Jesus was no doormat! Human love can only sacrifice "up to the point of pain", so we may read the chapter like this: "Love is patient (up to a point), Love doesn't take into account a suffered wrong (up to a point)."

For a fresh perspective, I encourage you to read it in the Message translation, but let me add a little more.

Love is messy. Love gets its hands dirty pulling others out of the mire. Love doesn't hold back because it sees someone's created value over the sin they're committing. Love dies to being insulted at the failed expectation of others, acknowledging who they are without nitpicking over what they're not. Love is willing to be hated for Truth until it melts a cold heart.

1 Peter 5:8 says the Devil is *seeking* whom he may devour. When lions are hunting, they look for weaknesses when thinning a herd because it makes the attack easier. The Devil does the same thing. If he could kill us at will, we'd all be dead. But, he is looking for a *strategic* kill; taking out one life that can cause hardness of heart in another towards God, knowing the slow poisoning of one can effect the sphere of the influence. This is a way of prolonging his imminent demise.

Frustration, anger, anxiety, and fear are merely a barometer on areas of our lives that have yet to be yielded to God in us. Neuroscientist Dr. Caroline Leaf said it best in her book, *Switch On Your Brain*, that "we are wired for love. When we choose other than that, we step into a fear zone, which contaminates our thinking and wires in toxic elements into our brain, producing death." Fear, not hate, is the opposite of love, and "perfect (complete, full-grown) love drives out fear" (1 John 4:18a AMP).

We have the ultimate weapon against frustration, anger, anxiety, and fear. So, when they raise their ugly heads, we can see them as attacks meant to steal love and begin to worship God for the revelation. Then, we can lay it before Him, become a living sacrifice, *wholly* acceptable unto Him.

Let's aspire to love without measure until we all reach oneness in the faith and in the knowledge of the Son of God, growing spiritually, to become mature believers, reaching to the measure of the fullness of Christ so that we are no longer spiritually immature (Ephesians 4:13)! The world will know us by our love, *so let's love hell out of people* and show them Jesus!

GRAB YOUR JOURNAL!

What is God showing you at this moment?

In light of this revelation, how does this shift your thoughts and actions?

God Doesn't Waste Anything

READ

Romans 8,

1 Corinthians 3:22,

1 Corinthians 3:3,

John 10:10,

Isaiah 2:3-5,

Isaiah 54:11-17,

2 Corinthians 3:2,

2 Corinthians 3:17,

Proverbs 4:18,

James 1:12

I often wonder about the things which have shaped me. My sense of humor came from my mom, my love for woodwork from my dad. My ability to make the best of bad situations came from watching my parents work through hard times. We know our ideas, attitudes, and abilities were formed in the way we were raised or through hardships we've endured or overcome. The question we need to answer is how are we going to allow those things (good or bad) to speak into our present.

1 Corinthians 3:22 (AMP, emphasis added) says, "... things *present* or things *to come*; all things are yours." If you read the entire scripture, you'll notice our past isn't mentioned because it doesn't belong to us. It was purchased with Jesus' blood, and it is *His* to do what He wants.

It would be illegal to take a joyride in a car I had sold just because I found a spare key, and it is also "illegal" for me to use a past which is no longer mine. It should no longer have the *authority* to speak into my life *or* shape my response. As born-again heirs to God's Kingdom and children of righteousness, we have a responsibility to walk differently than mere men (1 Corinthians 3:3). We are to renew our minds and see things in a new way (Romans 12:1-2).

Sometimes, we lend ourselves to vain reasoning, trying to validate our present feelings because of past abuse to give us ground to stand on. But, if we're standing on a lie because someone else who hurt us was *also* under the influence of a lie, we'll always be on shaky ground and perpetuating a cycle that God meant to destroy.

God doesn't cause bad things to happen to us (John 10:10), but He doesn't waste anything either. Isaiah 2:4 says He will cause us to beat our swords into plowshares and our spears into pruning hooks. Weapons we've either used or were once used against us will now work for us. They are now meant to be tools used for His harvest; the earth is groaning for the sons of God to reveal themselves (Romans 8:19)!

My definition of victory over the Devil entails taking all he tried to destroy me with and using it to drive him out (Isaiah 54:17).

Perseverance of faith brings one overcoming victory after another until we walk freely, unaffected by the voice of the Enemy. Let's allow Holy Spirit to take us from victim to conqueror, from slaves to sons and daughters, from glory to glory and faith to faith!

GRAB YOUR JOURNAL!

What is God showing you at this moment?

In light of this revelation, how does this shift your thoughts and actions?

What or Who is Shepherding You?

READ
Psalms 23,
1 Peter 2:25,
Ephesians 6:11-18,
James 1:5,
2 Peter 1:3,
Ephesians 4:27-30,
Isaiah 61:1-4,
Philippians 4:6-7,
Romans 12:12, 2
Corinthians 10:4-5,
1 John 5:14-15

Why God wakes me up at 3:30 a.m. praying or preaching in my sleep, I have no idea, but I'm coming to realize that He uses this time to show me areas I've ignored a little. While I'm sleeping may be the only time I hush long enough to process His thoughts instead of my own. When this recently happened, I had been dreaming I was ministering to a friend struggling with fear and depression. Compassion was flowing out of me as I was mentally ministering to him about meditating on God's Word as a strategy of warfare. God gave me Psalms 23, changing the words to prove a point:

Fear is my shepherd, so my eyes only see lack. It keeps me from green pastures, takes me through troubled waters and down paths of destruction. It ravages my soul, beating me with rods of accusation, stealing oil of joy from my anointing, making me feel that I am unworthy for the table God prepared for me. I live constantly in shadows of death. I feel totally alone. My cup is empty. Surely evil and cruelty follow me incessantly, barring me from God's presence forever.

He then said, "If you follow *anything* other than Me as Shepherd of your life, it will lead to this. So, why are you letting fear shepherd you?" I thought this was about my friend, but God was now turning to me, showing me where I was following fear masked as frustration.

He continued, "You wouldn't let a muddy pig run through your house or an enemy attack your family without a fight, so why are you allowing the Devil to steal your peace and violate your soul (your mind, will, and emotions)?

"You asked your friend what his strategy is but you have forgotten *Me* in this. Do you think you are resisting the Devil by turning inward and staying quiet?! All you're doing is packing it in deeper, and it will eat your peace like cancer. The Enemy is resisted through submission to Me. When you worship Me openly in the Enemy's presence, you remind him and yourself *Who I am* to you and *whose you are*! *The only time you need to let him see you sweat is in violent worship to Me, wielding the sword of the I Am.*"

Fear plants destructive thoughts like landmines from the Enemy which need to be disarmed before they cause huge damage. Prepare to confront our Enemy in battle by first putting on God's armor, like a bomb squad dressed in protective gear (Ephesians 6:11-18). Send out God's Word, through prayer, to unwrap and analyze the Devil's device, then diffuse it or detonate it in the safe place, the throne room of Heaven.

Let's examine our direction and what we're following by checking our worry level and the direction of our faith. What or whom are we following will be the evidence. Let's make a conscious effort to adjust and turn our hearts toward Christ, following after His lead.

GRAB YOUR JOURNAL!

What is God showing you at this moment?

In light of this revelation, how does this shift your thoughts and actions?

What's That Smell?

READ

2 Corinthians 3:1-3,

2 Corinthians 2:14-16,

1 Corinthians 1:18-19,

Romans 12:1,

1 Samuel 17,

Romans 8:1-16,

Daniel 3:16

"Well that just stinks!" is a phrase used when life throws a curveball. "The sweet smell of success," has been coined when we've been handed a win. When something is suspicious, it "smells fishy." Children who have no discipline are considered "spoiled rotten." In Isaiah 65:5 (NLT), God refers to rebellious people as a "stench" in His nostrils. 2 Corinthians 2:14 (AMP) says the God "who always leads us in triumph... spreads... the sweet fragrance of the knowledge of Him" through us. Our aroma is evident by those who are saved or those who are dying.

In the same way, aroma is released when fruit is cut or when the lid is lifted on a cooking pot, our lives and the fruit of our lips produce an aroma to those around us. As Christians, when we are cut by trials or cooked in tribulation, the aroma of Christ should be what is released.

Like it or not, everything we say and do is a testimony. But, it's the degree of our knowledge of Him and the awareness of our freedom which determines the aroma. We have been given the mind of Christ, though none of us have complete revelation of His mind. We don't know everything, but we are to walk in the light we have.

The Devil's job is to make us doubt what God has said, and he uses the pressures of life effectively. Matthew 13:21 says persecution comes because of the Word we receive. Whatever is planted is going to be tested. Most things we stumble over are what we've heard but failed to put into practice, so there is no deep root. When we are squeezed, why do we release frustration and anger instead of Christ?

While not every situation is our doing or our choice, our direction starts with our decision. We are to be living sacrifices, laying down what we value for what is more worthy. Is our unforgiveness worth the salvation of one who has betrayed us? Is our anger or frustration worth a loss of peace? We all have areas of our lives which are not fully surrendered. We were not created for self. If there's no sacrifice, there's no aroma. If there's no aroma, there's no testimony.

Like David the shepherd, when he killed a lion and a bear with the only witnesses being God and a few sheep, it's the private fight we win with no one watching that is to bring confidence for the public battles. Also like David, there will be those around us who either doubt, mock, or give advice. But, they are all watching. God is breathing in the fragrance of us under pressure, looking to show Himself through us.

When Shadrach, Meshach, and Abednego were thrown into the furnace, they had already determined their lives weren't about the size of the fire but about the size of their God. Whether He rescued them or not, their aroma would testify of His greatness.

Let's be filled with Christ and experience Him so deeply that no matter what our trial, His fragrance is breathed in by all who are watching, and we become a sweet aroma to our Father!

GRAB YOUR JOURNAL! | *What is God showing you at this moment?*

In light of this revelation, how does this shift your thoughts and actions?

Understanding Authority and Releasing Power!

READ

Psalms 50:23,

Mark 11:22-24,

Acts 3:1-12,

2 Corinthians 4:13,

John 7:37-39,

Joshua 1:8-9,

Isaiah 45:11,

Matthew 28:19-20,

Luke 10:18-20

When my daughter came home on terminal leave from the Marine Corps, she decided a puppy would be a good idea. So, Chooch Patucci, a ten-week-old, playful miniature Goldendoodle, has now graced us with *all* of his happiness. When he first arrived and was getting used to his surroundings, he became intimidated by an extremely dangerous *sock* lying on the den floor, from which came his very first bark ever. His own sound startled him so much, he ran over close to his new-found mama for protection. He has *since* found out how to *use* his bark.

"You do the same thing," I heard in my spirit. Holy Spirit instantly convicted my heart because there are some situations that have pressed *against* my faith and strong-armed me into retreat. If I couldn't see how a miracle could happen, I would pray as if *God* needed an *escape* if my prayer didn't work out. When my "bark" scared me, I retreated back to the safety of preserving self.

When we try to give God a "way out," praying safe prayers, we are actually trying to give ourselves a way out. We may think we are keeping God from looking bad if what we're praying for doesn't happen right away, but what we're actually doing is trying to save ourselves, which is pride. I say it often, "Holy Spirit is a big boy and can take care of Himself." When we get a revelation of who God is in us, who we are, and what we have *in Him*, we will release what is ours!

In Acts 3, Peter and John released what *they had* to a lame man, and he got up and walked. They didn't ask God to do anything! They simply said, "We don't have money, but what we do have, we'll give you. In the *name of Jesus*, get up and walk" (Acts 3:6, my paraphrase). They used the authority they were given and *released* Holy Spirit power. With everyone standing around marveling at what had just happened, Peter said, "Why are you staring at us, as though by our own power or godliness we had made this man walk" (Acts 3:12 AMP)?

It's His *revealed* word, which Holy Spirit makes alive in us, which has power! When we receive revelation, we go from *telling* what we've *heard*, to *showing* what we *know*. By speaking His Word with authority, power is released. If someone isn't healed when we pray, we don't accuse them of not having enough faith. We don't adjust the gospel to fit our experience. Jesus' life is our *only* comparison.

Jesus bought the right through His blood, to put healing power under *our* authority! Who are we to second guess His gift? We are to take our place as kings and priests. The priest stands before God, to fellowship, receive daily bread and orders of the day. We then go into our day as a king, taking that authority with us. We are neither beggars nor orphans. We are God's children.

Let's watch as the power behind the bark that once startled us, becomes the bark which intimidates the enemy. Let's be so full of living water, Holy Spirit simply flows out of us and onto others in our sphere of influence. The Word that's alive in us will be released from us!

GRAB YOUR JOURNAL!

What is God showing you at this moment?

In light of this revelation, how does this shift your thoughts and actions?

Free From a Slave Mentality

READ

Hebrews 5:11-14,

1 John 1:5-7,

Ephesians 5:1,

John 3:16,

1 John 4:7-8,

Matthew 6:33,

Luke 17:21,

Matthew 5:14-16,

John 15:14-16

One of my American heroes is Harriet Tubman, an escaped slave who became known as the "Moses of Her People." She conducted the Underground Railroad, leading slaves to freedom. She is often pictured with a gun that was meant for protection on the journey but also for anyone who became fearful and wanted to return. Harriet knew if they went back, the rest of the travelers would be at risk of being caught or killed. It is said she would pull out her gun and tell them, "You'll be free or die a slave!" Later, she said, "I never ran my train off the track, and I never lost a passenger."

She personally led around seventy people to freedom, but getting freedom inside someone is probably a little harder. After all, how does one change everything they've been to something they've never known? A free body doesn't necessarily mean a free mind, and often, we perpetuate it to the following generations. Breaking free from one's past life requires a new way of thinking, living, and walking. It requires new dreams, desires, and Godly fear above the fear of man.

As Christians, we understand that God has delivered us to restore us back to His full image. Jesus modeled perfect freedom, and He intends to not only bring us out of slavery, but fully remove us from sin (slave) consciousness. Yet, many in the church still come week after week to be fed milk from a pastor, produced after he ate the meat of revelation. All the while, God desires to feed *us* the meat of personal revelation (Hebrews 5:11-14).

If we're relying on someone else to spiritually feed us, we are living a substandard Christian life, hoping to earn favor, struggling to attain through our own efforts without learning to receive. Our adoption has given us every right that

Jesus had on this Earth. He expects us to live as a son who has just inherited Dad's Kingdom business and learn how to run it!

Our Heavenly Father does want to bless us but not with things which cause us to take Him for granted or destroy our love walk. Our blessings are meant to increase our dependency and relationship with Him. *Everything* He does is about the relationship. It's about learning to become a son or daughter. It's about Him living in us and a life of constant growth and transformation, from the inside to the outside, influencing everyone whose path we cross.

God has called us to walk in the light as He is in the light, that our hearts be flooded with light. He has called us to imitate Christ and become light to those who walk in darkness. We become trusted confidants who see, comprehend, and become one with the heart of our King.

Let's get rid of the slave mentality keeping us from pursuing the Kingdom we have been given to explore through faith. Let's shed the beliefs we have created from our feelings and allow Holy Spirit to teach us His ways. Let's begin to enlarge our territory for our Father's glory. When we seek Him with all of our hearts, we will live in constant revelation as His children on a love assignment from the throne!

GRAB YOUR JOURNAL! | *What is God showing you at this moment?*

In light of this revelation, how does this shift your thoughts and actions?

Come Up Here!

READ

Job 1:9-11,

2 Corinthians 4:17,

Revelation 4:1,

Ephesians 2:1-10,

James 1:2-11,

Romans 8:31-39

In 1989, Robin Williams starred as Professor Keating in the movie *Dead Poets Society*. I don't necessarily recommend the movie based on some of the content, but one scene, in particular, has stuck with me.

Keating, in the hopes of inspiring his class of teenage boys to enjoy poetry, jumps up on his desk, encouraging his class to see from different perspectives. He invites them all to give it a try so they too can see how the view is entirely different when you are standing above.

It's easy to get caught up in our fishbowl world, with all of our internal struggles and external circumstances. Turning inward may cause us to miss out on God's point of view. As we go through valleys, we may feel the mountainside closing in on us, shutting out the Light. We might lose sight of Whose we are and why we're here. We may begin to wonder where God is and if He cares. When that happens, we have fallen right into the Enemy's plan to keep us shadowed in isolation, so busy struggling that we get cut off from our commission.

Whatever hell we have been through or are going through, our affliction has nothing to do with who we are or God's love for us (2 Corinthians 4:17). Our response to our circumstances reveals to us the direction of our faith.

Check out Job 1:9-11. When Satan attacked Job, he (Satan) basically told God, "The only reason he [Job] worships you is because you've blessed him. If I touch his life, he'll curse You." Satan is still saying this about God's children today. But, what if when Satan pushes us, instead of causing us to question God or our identity as His dear child, he pushes us right into God's arms, further anchoring our faith?

What if we understand that we are not limited to our perspective but are invited to see things from the Throne of Heaven? When St. John wrote the book of Revelation, God told him, *"Come up here* and I will show you…"* (Revelation 4:1 NIV, emphasis added). Ephesians 2:6 (AMP, emphasis added) says Jesus "seated us *with Him in the heavenly places*," so why do we choose to look only with our natural eyes? By omitting God from the equation, we lose out on a more complete truth, shortchanging ourselves of the blessings which come with a heavenly perspective, or we gauge God's love based on our circumstances.

James 1:2-4 (AMP) tells us to consider trials as a source of joy because they produce endurance that leads us to inner peace, patience, and maturity *if we keep our focus* on our faith in Christ. Verses 7 and 8 go on to say, "For such a person ought not to think or expect that he will receive anything [at all] from the Lord, being a double-minded man, unstable and restless in all his ways [in everything he thinks, feels, or decides]."

It is impossible for us to walk two different directions simultaneously. It is impossible to attain anything if we wear ourselves out floundering between faith and fear.

The Devil uses tribulation to keep us from understanding our power and identity, so he can keep his hold on this earth a little longer.

Let's get our perspective from the throne! Let's be wise to our Enemy and his devices and stand firm in our faith. Let's determine once and for all, that no matter what he's tried to kill, steal, and destroy in us, we will focus on one thing: We are God's children and *nothing* can separate us from His love!

GRAB YOUR JOURNAL! | *What is God showing you at this moment?*

In light of this revelation, how does this shift your thoughts and actions?

Just One Door

READ

Romans 3:20,

Matthew 16:24-26,

John 14:6,

John 10:1-18,

3 John 2,

Romans 6:23,

Matthew 13:16-23,

Matthew 7:13-14,

Psalms 23,

2 Corinthians 10:4-6,

Jeremiah 29:11,

Psalms 91

Jesus said in Revelation 3:20 (NKJV, emphasis added), "Behold I stand at the door and knock." There is one door, the heart. Everything we say or do, how we see and understand comes from it. If we close the door to forgiveness, it can neither give nor receive it. If the door is closed, we may believe we are keeping evil at bay. But, we *fail* to see we have locked ourselves in a prison of our own making. In holding back any part of our lives from God in order to preserve it, we never experience life in abundance nor have the opportunity to see faith bring results.

While Jesus was explaining Heaven to His disciples, they asked how they could know the way to where He was going. He said, "I am *the* way, *the* truth, and *the* life. No one comes to the Father except *through me*" (John 14:6 NIV, emphasis added).

In John 10, Jesus explained He, Himself, is the Door by which we enter (John 10:9-10). Anyone coming over the wall, or by some other way, is a thief. Of course, He is talking about eternal salvation, but salvation is about more than our spirits getting to Heaven. It's about getting Heaven into us! Salvation is for our souls, which includes our mind, will, and emotions. The way is narrow, but once we are through the Door, the pastures where He leads are endless (Matthew 7:13-14, Psalms 23:2)!

When we are born again, we are instantly spiritually saved and going to Heaven. Salvation is a free gift (Romans 6:23)! However, how we choose to explore the benefits of this gift will determine the prosperity of our souls here on Earth (Matthew 13:21). How we respond to Holy Spirit, who is our Comforter, Advocate, Intercessor, Counselor, Strengthener, and Standby, determines the depth He is able to influence our lives. Circumstances may not always be favorable, but if we are rooted and grounded in His love, He will guide us through life's hard places (1 John 4:18).

So, we need to identify the thieves coming over the walls or through the cracks who are stealing from our souls. What is stealing our joy or our God-purchased victory, vision, or passion? What thief is *dividing* us from others so we're easy targets? Have they *paid a price* to have the authority to speak into our lives, to shepherd us? Are they invested in our future? To be sure, thieves won't stick around when the devourer comes nor stand with us on the day of judgment to qualify us before God.

We are constantly bombarded with thoughts and feelings. Some good. Some bad. Some are merely judgment calls. But, the qualifier for receiving or rejecting them is they *must only* come through the door- *Jesus Christ*. We can't allow the opinions of man to sneak over the fence trying to outweigh the Word of God or allow the thief to steal from us. We are not to be lured away by our emotions and become a god unto ourselves. Let's decide whom we are serving and *who we are becoming* as we lean in to hear Him and stop the thief from coming over the wall!

GRAB YOUR JOURNAL!

What is God showing you at this moment?

In light of this revelation, how does this shift your thoughts and actions?

Eating With Jesus

READ

Matthew 6:6,

John 14:26,

Revelation 3:19-22,

2 Timothy 3:16 (TPT),

Ephesians 2:6-7,

1 John 4:17,

Romans 8:37-39

Have you ever invited someone over for dinner spur of the moment and rushed home ahead of them to clean? In a mad dash, we throw the pile of laundry in the laundry room, put a couple of things in our bedroom, *and shut the door.* Conquering the clutter, we want to make a good impression and enjoy our guest without distraction.

There's a famous painting by Warner Sallman called "Christ at Heart's Door," based on Revelation 3:20. It depicts Jesus standing at our door, knocking, waiting to share in a feast with us. I wonder if behind the door He is knocking on, someone is scrambling to throw things in rooms and closets before they open the door for Him. In Sunday School, we were taught it was the door of salvation, but I think it means so much more.

Matthew 6:6 (AMP) says, "... when you pray, go into your most private room, *close the door* and pray to your Father who is in secret..." (emphasis added). Often, we go to prayer and leave Jesus standing outside knocking. We spew out our needs and thoughts for the day but may never pause to receive empowerment, seek direction on matters, or allow Him to express His heart for our lives. It's when we *shut the door on the wandering thoughts* and are deliberate about our honored Guest, that we *open the door to Him.* When we get past the superficial lists and guilt-ridden apologies, we enter the secret place where we truly connect. Love is perfected in us in union and fellowship with Holy Spirit (1 John 4:17). To enter the secret place, we close the door on our own thoughts and plans, our anxieties, how we feel about ourselves, and get *intentionally focused on* His Presence in the moment. We partner with Him to gain wisdom, learn strategies, and receive power that we may be the *visible display* of Jesus and His anointing!

John 14:26 says Holy Spirit is our Helper. The Amplified Bible defines Helper as "Comforter, Advocate, Intercessor—Counselor, Strengthener, Standby." It's only right to have Him join us in prayer.

Holy Spirit stands ready to empower us through instruction and correction, giving us the strength to take the right direction and leading us deeper into the path of godliness (2 Timothy 3:16). He wants to train us to eagerly pursue what is right; for the *ones who conquer*, He will give the privilege of sitting with Him on His throne. If our hearts are open, we will hear what the Spirit is saying right now (Revelation 3:19-22).

It may take a little practice, but Holy Spirit is with us to help. So, let's quickly close the door on all the distractions in our mind, open the door of our hearts to Him and let the feast begin!

GRAB YOUR JOURNAL!

What is God showing you at this moment?

In light of this revelation, how does this shift your thoughts and actions?

Love Doesn't Mean the Absence of Conflict

READ

Hebrews 12:11,

1 Corinthians 3:1-15,

Proverbs 13:24,

2 Timothy 3:16,

1 Corinthians 13:1-8

(MSG),

Mark 2:13-17 (AMP)

A toddler and his mom were entering the locker area of the gym where I work out. He had a rock he'd found in the parking lot, and when mom had her back turned, he kicked it into the stand-up mirror. Luckily, it didn't break, but it was loud enough to startle her. She scooped him up, corrected him properly, and took the rock away, to which he replied through tears, "You mean! You hurt my feelings! You not my friend!" I just kind of giggled as she talked him through his manipulative tears. Then she told me, "That's the first time he's ever said that to me. It kinda breaks my heart." Yep. Welcome to toddlerhood! It's hard not to want them to be happy, but doing so just to avoid conflict will only produce spoiled children who don't know how to handle correction and discipline.

Love doesn't mean an absence of conflict. Love actually invests in it. Love is willing to take the emotional hits because it is looking to develop something greater through relationship. God is willing to do the same; He goes after whatever stands in the way between He and us.

What the child saw as "mean" was a loving discipline that said, "I love you too much to allow you to continue this behavior. I love you too much to allow these thought processes to become habits that will create rebellion against truth." Proverbs 13:24 (AMP) says, "He who withholds the rod [of discipline] hates his son, But he who loves him disciplines *and* trains him diligently *and* appropriately [with wisdom and love]."

No healthy person enjoys strife. How great it would be to avoid all confrontation. If it weren't for *other* people, our "fruit of the Spirit" would be weighing down our vines! But, relationships will show us *just* how much we need to grow in love. Navigating situations with love is the challenge. When operating in love, we must be fully committed to seeing the best outcome, while also pruning selfish motives that arise (and they *will* raise their ugly heads).

We must remember that sin is a result of a deeper issue. Rebellion manifests when the enemy blinds people to the truth of their created value. People build mental walls to rationalize their choices, to create a sense of peace, even when they are in blatant rebellion to God. Most will go to great lengths to protect that false peace when it is challenged.

Jesus was a magnet for sinners. He loved and accepted people in spite of but without condoning sin. Our love for Jesus and people should be the first thing people see about us. Without this love, we are no more than loud, clanging cymbals, sounding more like protesters than Heaven's ambassadors. We cannot live offended by people who are in sin, deceived by darkness. They deserve our prayers because Christ's valuable blood was shed for their salvation. We must learn to respond to what God is saying, rather than react to what the Devil is doing.

Let's learn to seek God for His wisdom, content to plant and water, allowing God to give the increase, prayerfully interceding for those who need an advocate, so we attract those in darkness to His Light like Jesus did (Mark 2:16-17).

GRAB YOUR JOURNAL!

What is God showing you at this moment?

In light of this revelation, how does this shift your thoughts and actions?

Contend for the Faith

READ

Galatians 6:7-9,

Jude 3,

Matthew 6:33,

Mark 16:15-20,

James 1:5-8,

Romans 10:17,

John 14:26,

Matthew 6:6,

1 Corinthians 14:1,

1 Corinthians 13:11-13

Have you ever thought there was something keeping God from hearing your prayer? You try to reason, "If I just pray harder… longer… more intently… God will hear me." Or, "Maybe I'm not worthy enough, so I'll try harder to live better." We can wind up creating doctrines to live by to temporarily satisfy our minds while stifling the longing in our hearts, or we may live with the constant guilt of never living "good enough" to satisfy God, and neither of these are true.

Why do we often learn to live with less instead of contending for more? We have to realize we're not trying to get God to change His mind. 3 John 2 (KJV, emphasis added) says, "Beloved, I wish above all things that thou mayest *prosper and be in health...*" so we know His will is for our best.

Our mind searches for a thought to rest on, so we sometimes create a logic which brings temporary satisfaction. My definition of faith includes being satisfied to live in the unknown, knowing the Comforter in the midst of an uncomfortable situation. While God wants us to have our miracle, He also wants to instill and settle our knowledge of our identity in Him, but we need to understand that one is not necessarily contingent on the other.

Miracles are gifts to us, but they are not our destination. Our destiny is fulfilled when we decide to walk into what God is showing us, even when our experience seems to contradict His promise. We must not allow circumstances of any kind to distract us from seeking *first* the kingdom of God (Matthew 6:33) and believing God (Mark 16:17-18) without wavering (James 1:6-8).

There are times when we are to come into God's presence and contend with things which are working against us or our situation. But, this life is all about *relationship*, knowing who our Father is and knowing we have the same rights as sons (Romans 8:29 AMP).

We rightly desire miraculous power working through us. We do everything we can to make a miracle happen with the best of intentions. But, if miracles came simply out of highly focused prayer, it would be a work of the flesh with no faith applied, and we would either take credit for it or create a doctrine of it.

Faith comes by hearing, through His Word, what God is saying. Then, we *only* say what He said. We keep seeking God, first and foremost, to become intimately acquainted with Him, falling head-over-heels in love. We'll be so full of Him until He's ready to bust out of us and all over those around us!

Press in, keep it pure and simple, and *don't give up*!

GRAB YOUR JOURNAL!

What is God showing you at this moment?

In light of this revelation, how does this shift your thoughts and actions?

Freedom From Manipulation

READ
Romans 12:14-21,
Philippians 4:5-9,
Romans 6:15-17,
1 Peter 5:5-11,
James 4:6 (AMP),
Luke 23:34,
1 Corinthians 13,
Romans 13:8-10,
Psalms 62:8,
Romans 8:31-37

There are people who have left a negative impact on our lives. We may avoid them, hold grudges, act in a passive-aggressive way towards them, or politely grit our teeth while they are in our presence. We may filter our intentions, not wanting other people to hurt, so we try to *fix* things, *which can still be a form* of manipulation. Whatever the method, the heart reveals itself. For personal safety, some people may need to be avoided, but we should always pray for God to send ministers to them and shower them with spiritual blessing. For, God has called us to love our enemies and overcome evil with good.

If we become offended, guilt-driven, and hurt, our Father has two kids to correct— us and them. If our response is to let someone know how bad they've hurt us through emotional rebuttal, then we are practicing manipulation, which speaks to our immaturity or our own willfulness.

When something hurts us, we may be inclined to dive headfirst into an emotional whirlpool, which sucks us under. If we continue to allow the pain to dominate our thinking, we can end up feeling guilty for walking in unforgiveness. We might stuff our pain in the back of our mind, merely throwing a scripture on it as if we've checked it off a list, not allowing His words to penetrate and heal our hearts. Our progressive guilt-spiral can hinder us from complete communion with Holy Spirit, which leads to feelings of hopelessness, deceiving us into thinking we are defeated in a battle which Christ has already won for us. These actions *resist* God's grace. What does this say about *us*, if He gives grace to the *humble*?

We often seek an absence of conflict, but this is a false peace. We have to step out of our own way and allow Holy Spirit to handle His kids. God desires us to be comfortable in uncomfortable situations (Philippians 4:5-7). Why else would we need a Comforter?

We cannot afford to be hurt, defeated Christians, fashioned by anything other than Christ. Neither can we buy favor trying to gain acceptance. Romans 13:8 (AMP) says, "Owe nothing to anyone except to love *and* seek the best for one another;..." and that unselfish love fulfills the command to love our neighbor as we do ourselves. Those hurt feelings are distractions thrown in our path to keep us from running the race set before us and are roadblocks to becoming love.

We pour out our cares and feelings before Him, but we must also allow Him to pour back into us the grace to overcome. We suffer long. We love. We serve. We give. But never from compulsion or obligation. While we mourn for those who are deceived, it is equally deceptive for us to be anything less than who we are in Christ (1 Corinthians 13).

Setting aside our emotions can feel like dying. It is! According to Paul, we are to take up our cross and follow Jesus. We are to die daily. We must continue to remember that we are *becoming love*. We are imitating God and becoming more like our Father every day.

GRAB YOUR JOURNAL!

What is God showing you at this moment?

In light of this revelation, how does this shift your thoughts and actions?

We Were Worth Leaving Heaven For

READ

2 Corinthians 5:14-21,

Philippians 2:7-9,

Romans 8:29-30,

Luke 19:10,

Matthew 6:19-34,

Genesis 1:28,

Matthew 28:19

I can remember my grandmother longing for Heaven because of the struggles of life. She was taught in church the world is evil and bad, and one day God will rescue us out of it. She lived, trusting God in the midst of worry, but at the mercy of the Enemy and circumstances. Like many believers, she never realized the potential she carried, even though she loved Jesus and did good Christian things her entire life.

God didn't send Jesus, His only begotten Son, simply to take us to Heaven. He intended Heaven to get into us. There is a huge difference. He is not just on a rescue mission. He is on a mission of transformation as the world changes through the growth of His kingdom, *through the salvation of each of us!* Jesus didn't die because we were a bunch of crummy sinners. He died to restore *that* which was lost, which was our value, calling, purpose, and destiny. He died because *Our Father loves us and wants more for us than we deserve*!

He was willing to become human flesh with the same limitations we have (Philippians 2:7-9), so He could restore us to who we were intended to be—Children of God in the image of Christ (Romans 8:29)! If He died so we may live, we should live as He would, in unison and purpose with our Father!

2 Corinthians 5:14-15 says if one died so that everybody else might live, then those who live shouldn't live for themselves. This means we no longer judge people at face value, or for what they are producing, or failing to produce. We are to see them according to their destiny, their created value, and their potential for Christ.

We were created to expand Eden to cover the Earth, putting everything in order and tending it. When Adam messed up, God already had a plan in place. Rather than scrap the idea, He did what was necessary to restore us back to Himself! Sin stole man's heart from God, so He paid the price to get it back.

God created a garden in the untamed expanse of Earth, and gave Adam the task of expanding its order and his dominion. Now, we are deep in the chaos of untamed people, with the garden of Heaven inside us, and we are meant to expand its dominion and order to the hearts of all (Genesis 1:28)! Often, we are unaware of our identity and authority made available in Christ and remain powerless in those areas (Hosea 4:6).

Once we understand our identity, our destiny is empowered. There is no lack because we have all the resources of Heaven at our disposal. We are not to live at the mercy of our circumstances, politics, race, or denominations! If our eyes are on those things, we need to change and ask to see through His eyes. Matthew 6 says that if our eye is focused on Him alone, our entire body will be flooded with light! That means, if our eyes are distracted by what we lack, how bad things are, or what we're *not*, then we allow darkness to overshadow us, living less than He intended!

Let's singly focus our vision on God, so that every day our purpose is to *re-present* what our Father looks like to those in our circle of influence; not whining and complaining, but Kingdom-minded, and mission-oriented. Let's *go* and make disciples, y'all!

GRAB YOUR JOURNAL!

What is God showing you at this moment?

In light of this revelation, how does this shift your thoughts and actions?

Got Peace?

READ

Matthew 6:25-34,

Proverbs 3:5-10,

Proverbs 3:13-27,

John 14:25-27 (AMP),

1 Corinthians 1:18-25,

Psalms 16:11,

Ephesians 2:14,

James 4:1-6,

Romans 14:17-19

I saw a piece of artwork at a store which read, "Peace is not about silence. It is not a place without trouble or fear. Peace is standing in the middle of chaos and finding the calm in your heart."

So often we, as Christians, mimic those in the world who are striving for *peace*. We look to relationships, medication, food, sports, TV, education, money, yoga, vacation, or some hobby or activity to find what has been purchased by Christ's blood and offered through Holy Spirit. There's nothing wrong with distractions except when we give them the place reserved for God. We find things containing an *element* of peace, and we think we've found peace in them, but it is temporary. Seeking peace in the external will actually stir conflict with our spirit (James 4:1).

When the diet is blown, our team loses, the meds wear off, or vacation is over, the peace is gone. On the flip side, we sometimes force ourselves to stop caring about things to the degree we confuse peace with indifference. If nothing is disturbing us, we think we have peace.

If we look at the life of Jesus, we notice He threw Himself into less than peaceful situations, yet remained at peace internally. He upset, challenged, and often offended people's senses to wake them to the condition of their hearts. Then He could *bring* the peace they so desired.

Every heart and mind desires peace as its core. Haggai 2:7 (KJV) prophesied the "desire of all nations shall come." Ephesians 2:15 says Jesus *is* our peace, though many don't know it is Him they seek. Righteousness, peace, and joy are *in* Holy Spirit (Romans 14:17). The world desires the *gift* without the Giver, but

He's a package deal. The gift of Holy Spirit dwelling in us brings with Him all the things our heart really desires.

Peace begins with *"Thy kingdom come"* (Matthew 6:10 KJV, emphasis added), and *"Seek ye first the kingdom"* (Mathew 6:33 KJV, emphasis added), and "Christ, the *power* of God and the *wisdom* of God" (1 Corinthians 1:24 KJV, emphasis added). If we desire real peace, we must seek Christ above the inferior distractions which give temporary peace, but hinder true, internal peace.

Proverbs 3:16 says wisdom carries certain gifts in Her left and right hand. Why chase after the provisions in one hand when we're invited to run smack into Jesus and allow both hands to embrace us? Our real desire is only found in intimacy with Him. If we keep looking to the King to be the Kings of our hearts, we'll find the peace we desperately desire (Ephesians 2:14).

GRAB YOUR JOURNAL!

What is God showing you at this moment?

In light of this revelation, how does this shift your thoughts and actions?

Trying or Being?

READ

Psalms 46:10,

James 2:14-26,

Ephesians 2:8,

Romans 5:15-21,

Luke 5:17,

Hebrews 6:19,

Hebrews 11:6

As a young Christian, I was intent on following after God's Word, as I should've been. I would implement sermons and scriptures in my life to feel better about my imperfect heart. Comparison became my measuring stick. If I was performing *poorly*, I felt condemned, and if I was doing *well*, I became judgmental. I was fully persuaded His ways were right, but I struggled with consistency. I was doing works without a lot of faith. I didn't know how to *receive* His grace and rest in His love and *just be His.*

Often we struggle with faith because we're trying to do Holy Spirit's job or tell Him how to do it. We put on a good front, but inwardly, we're hurt, angry, or anxious Christians, handling things on our own while quoting scripture, trying to convince ourselves we're trusting God. So, many disgruntled Christians who feel God failed to bring the desired result of all their efforts, fall into the deception of "*been* there, *done* that, *didn't* work for me."

God's grace is always available, though not always received. When we release faith, we open ourselves to receive the grace always flowing in our direction. By grace (God's empowering favor) we are saved (rescued, restored). If there's no faith, there's no grace. Look at it this way: faith is the door grace comes through. If there's no submission of our heart, there's no place for grace to enter. We may start out in faith, but when God doesn't show up on our time or according to our expectation, doubt and unbelief short-circuit the power of grace on our behalf. Sometimes our faith is in our expectations and timelines rather than in Him.

We all have times when we're in emergency mode when we feel God must answer us NOW! That's when the problem seems bigger than God. Whenever we are feeling pressured by life, it's a good idea to keep our eyes focused and heart submitted by praying something like this:

"God, I understand You didn't make me to be inwardly focused and driven by every emotional whim. I wasn't made to live by my senses or strength. I give myself to You and thank You for making me a person of faith. I lay my life on Your altar so I may declare and glorify Your Name to those in my sphere of influence. Thank You that when they see me encounter trials or notice my flaws, they will see You at work in me. Your *Grace* is with me, and You *sit* on the throne of my heart. I esteem *You* above my own opinions and thoughts. I thank You for readjusting my emotions. I praise You that Your blood redeemed me. I am not broken, busted, nor disgusted, but full of Your joy and life. Today, my eye is one with Yours, and I thank You that *Your love* rules my heart!"

The way we move from our self-centered desires, which keep us striving to manipulate situations, people, or God, is to be fully persuaded in our submission to His love for us which comes through intimacy and communion. We don't have to respond and react the way the world does. We can adjust our hearts daily to just *be* His child in the secret place so He supernaturally spills over into the outflow of our lives.

GRAB YOUR JOURNAL!

What is God showing you at this moment?

In light of this revelation, how does this shift your thoughts and actions?

The Word and His Voice

READ

1 Corinthians 2:13-15,

John 5:39-47,

Malachi 3:6,

John 8:31-32,

Philippians 2:12,

Revelation 2:7,

Romans 10:14-17,

John 10:27-29,

Psalms 32:8-10,

Ecclesiastes 3:1-11

Do you ever have one of those moments where just as soon as you think you have God figured out or think you know what you're supposed to do about something, you find out He's going in a different direction? You might even wonder if God changed His mind.

Do we fight and intercede or sit still and wait? Are we supposed to be the warrior or the child? The king or the priest?

We see it throughout the Bible. In one instance, God tells His people to fight, and in the next, to stand still and let Him fight for them. One reference tells us the kingdom of Heaven is to be taken violently in faith (Matthew 11:12), and another tells us to receive it as a little child (Mark 10:15).

It's no wonder those outside the Kingdom have trouble understanding God's Word. The Word of God without the presence of God shaping and increasing love in us, interpreting for us through Holy Spirit, can be a dangerous thing. We're not looking for *rules* when we read His Word, but *His voice* filling our hearts. Those who read the Bible looking for a scripture they can obey so they can have a form of religion emulating what they think Christianity should look like, only become religious and proud, often demanding others line up with *their* lifestyle.

When we read God's Word, we must listen to what the Spirit is saying *in the moment*. His voice will never contradict His Word, but it will test our faith. There are times we fight, and there are times we rest. There are some times where we give everything, and there are other times we store up our resources. There are times we fast and times we are to celebrate with feasting.

While the truths of God never change, and while we are to seek truth and love in all things, the path He chooses to bring us into truth is rarely defined. It's because He wants an intimate relationship with us. He has a way prepared for us, and life is found in Holy Spirit's divine influence on our hearts.

God is not a formula nor is prayer an incantation. "In Jesus' Name" is not the abracadabra to make miracles happen. The Pharisees were zealous for the scripture, but Jesus quickly let them know they had missed the point. The scriptures pointed to Himself, yet they didn't recognize Him. They thought that life was in the keeping of scripture, but in their activity, they had missed out on the relationship which brings life.

Faith comes by *hearing*. Revelation 2:7 (TPT, emphasis added) says, "The one whose heart is open let him *listen carefully* to what the Spirit is *saying...*" Jesus said His sheep would know *His voice* not just words on a page.

Let's tune in to hear His whispers to our heart with faith in *expecting* to hear. He is *always talking*. Let's thank Him for His love, a hearing heart, understanding, and for leading us to intensify our relationship with Him! He's excitedly waiting to talk to us!

GRAB YOUR JOURNAL!

What is God showing you at this moment?

In light of this revelation, how does this shift your thoughts and actions?

Storm Damage and Hope

READ

John 10:10,

John 15:3,

Hebrews 12:28,

Hebrews 11:1-3,

Psalms 18:25-36,

Psalms 40:1-5,

Jude 1:17-25,

Psalms 138:3,

Psalms 89:21,

Hebrews 13:9

With all of the damage from Hurricane Matthew in our area, I felt both saddened and blessed. While many were being evacuated from their homes, some of us only had to deal with the inconveniences of leaky roofs, no electricity, no place to shower, and traffic rerouted because of washed-out roads.

Fortunately, camping had prepared our family for cooking outdoors or, more importantly for me, how to steep coffee over an open flame. Years earlier, Hurricanes Fran and Hugo had taught us to fill the tub with water so we could flush our toilets and fill gallon jugs for drinking. We learned to top off our vehicles and containers with gas and to have a generator to keep ours and our neighbors' deep-freezers cold, and, of course, a chainsaw to help those with fallen trees.

God revealed a spiritual connection to me with this hurricane. Storms of different magnitudes reveal weaknesses. Hurricane Matthew showed us the weakness of our sandy ground, which is great for helping water to recede but not stable enough for flowing water. Once the earth beneath them was saturated, roads that had been designed to hold massive weight began to shift with the rushing water and washed away from beneath. Engineers rebuilt them with this in mind for the next storm.

Spiritual storms can help us discover areas to build a stronger spiritual infrastructure or train for the next battle. Temporary setbacks and stall-outs may cause us to misplace our faith momentarily, but whether experiencing a tropical storm or a hurricane, we were never designed to lose hope. Having been born again, we look to see a different kingdom and have seen far too many miracles to be mere coincidence. So, even if we die in battle, we still win. Hope is what our faith clings to, and our hope is *in* our Lord.

The Bible's definition of hope is the confident expectation of God using all for good and His glory. Good will come out of natural disaster. In Fayetteville's case, bridges will be rebuilt to withstand the next great storm. Roads will be reinforced with better underlayment. When we experience "washout" from storms, weak places are revealed in us. We are to build ourselves up in faith (Jude 20), to strengthen ourselves in God like David (1 Samuel 30:6), so we can preserve ourselves in the next storm.

Intimately knowing our Father eliminates our right to give up or to live discouraged. If our hope is, indeed, in the Lord, it's impossible. It's only when our eyes are looking at storms from our perspective instead of His, that our faith becomes misplaced. He has given us the keys to the kingdom. He has placed His kingdom at hand. His kingdom cannot be shaken.

Storms are going to come. Things are not going to go as planned. We will experience loss, but we must guard our hearts. Above all, we should quit focusing on what we think we've lost and instead find peace in worship to Him. Let's learn from past storms how to maneuver the next one so we won't be blown off our course, whether in the natural or spiritual realm. The God of restoration and increase is *our* Father.

GRAB YOUR JOURNAL!

What is God showing you at this moment?

In light of this revelation, how does this shift your thoughts and actions?

Faith and Authority

READ

2 Timothy 3:1-17,

Galatians 5:7-12,

Mark 4:13-20,

Mark 4:35-41,

Psalms 16:8,

Matthew 11:28-30,

Proverbs 14:12,

Romans 8:1,

Isaiah 61:3,

1 Corinthians 13:13,

Hebrews 12:2,

Galatians 2:20,

Matthew 28:18-20

When our kids were smaller, we would take them fishing off the coast of North Carolina in the inlet waterways and just beyond. Our boat was dwarfed in relation to the ships passing us. The massive barges moved so slowly they didn't even cast a wake, but some of the sport fishermen, showing off their triple outboard motors, blazed by us so fast it would nearly rock us off our feet.

I can only imagine what it must have been like for the disciples in the real storm like the one in Mark 4:35-41. And Jesus had fallen asleep! He had to have been exhausted because there is no other way one could sleep being slung side-to-side with water washing into the boat. Being experienced fishermen, Peter and John had probably traversed rough water before, but when the storm began to act like it had a personal vendetta toward them, fear took over. They had done all they knew to do, but weariness and worry had settled in. Tired and overcome, they woke Jesus. "*Don't you care* that we're going to die?"

Jesus knew His mission was waiting on the other side and knew there was no force that could stop it. After He rebuked the storm, He turned to them and asked, "*Why were you afraid?*"

God has given us *all* authority (Luke 10:19). Many times, we just don't exercise it. We may get overtaken by the size of the storm, the waves rocking our boat, and the water pouring in. So, we pray, speaking His Word like it's some kind of incantation and think when something doesn't happen, it's either not God's will or we don't have enough faith (which is condemnation *not* found in Christ [Romans 8:1]).

Sometimes, we tend to reduce our faith to our experience, moved by what we are feeling or seeing. We get caught up in the "why's" and let the questions squish the faith right out of us. We do religious things which seem right but don't bring life. We succumb to a spirit of heaviness in our weariness.

God means for our faith to be strong and enduring. But to do so, it *must be exercised*. Forces are going to come against us! It is not *always* going to be easy. 2 Timothy 3 says we will suffer for our faith (2 Timothy 3:10-14). We have seen Christians in the United States and abroad suffer various degrees of persecution because of convictions they refuse to compromise. We may even be misunderstood by "religious" people who don't really *know* God (Galatians 5:7-12).

God is the Author and Finisher of our faith (Hebrews 12:2). It is His faith in us which does the work (Galatians 2:20). But, if faith doesn't cling to hope which is attached to love (God is Love), which is the greatest force and weapon of all, we will be like a withering branch, cut off from its source, and we will grow weary in well-doing.

Let's establish ourselves in love, first and foremost, knowing we are loved by our Father God, and His Holy Spirit chooses to live in us! Then, faith will have something to cling to in the storms we are heading for!

GRAB YOUR JOURNAL! | *What is God showing you at this moment?*
In light of this revelation, how does this shift your thoughts and actions?

Don't Partner with Fear

READ

Hebrews 4:15,

Joshua 1:6-9,

Psalms 23 (TPT),

Revelation 12:10-12,

2 Corinthians 12:9-10

Most of us have experienced or done things which have negatively directed our lives. Abuse, misunderstanding, or bad life choices produce results we have to live with. God already knows these things, yet He still loves us and has a plan for us in spite of it all. He still intends for us to walk in victory *in the midst* of our struggles. He expects us to love and forgive without fear. We may feel like there is no way to overcome these feelings. We may have fought hard to build a wall of strength to protect ourselves from pain and weakness, hiding the truth from those around us.

Too often our one failure or fear picks at us like a child does a scab; threatens us when we try to make better choices and is liable to keep us from healing completely. By protecting what we've built, we may sabotage ourselves, our relationships, or even God's plan for our lives.

God created us in His image and gave us our feelings, but He didn't intend for us to live by them. If we are led by them, they can become our god. It's okay to acknowledge fear, as a response to a situation, but when we partner with it, coming into agreement with it, we become slaves to it.

Love and fear stand in opposition to each other, and the life choices we make are based on one or the other. Fear produces feelings which can resonate so loudly in our body, drowning out the Word of Truth because it is focused on preserving those walls we've built called reputation, dignity, and comfort.

All throughout God's Word, He has reminded people to be strong and courageous. We would not have to show courage if there was no element of fear to push past. In the command to take courage, He creates the provision for us to overcome. He is telling us, "Yes, this is scary to the person who doesn't have

Me with them. But *I am with you!*" Then, He invites us to sit at His banquet table of grace and strength and eat provision while the enemy watches (Psalms 23:5).

Satan is empowered in our lives through our agreement with fear, which is why he uses our feelings to keep us off balance. But, he cannot keep us dislocated in our effectiveness if we don't partner with him in fear. Revelation 12:11 says we conquered him completely through the blood of the Lamb and the powerful word of His testimony. We triumphed because they (we) did not love and cling to their (our) own lives, even when faced with death (my paraphrase).

Let's praise God for the fact that our past cannot and will not define us! Our past can no longer hurt us when we see it as a trophy of what we've overcome in Christ. Now, we are free and empowered to be all that He has called us to be!

GRAB YOUR JOURNAL!

What is God showing you at this moment?

In light of this revelation, how does this shift your thoughts and actions?

Hopeful New Year!

READ

Hebrews 6:19,

Hebrews 11:1,

Psalms 20,

Romans 12:1-2,

1 Corinthians 13:13, 1

Corinthians 13:1-3,

Hebrews 12:1-3,

2 Corinthians 3:2

How did you view your previous year? We live in a dramatic and historic, world-rocking, culture-shaking time! Whether you've experienced tragedy, loss, or disappointment, you've probably had some wonderful moments as well. How do you anticipate the coming year? Do you sense hopelessness or an expectation of the manifestation of God's Word? The simple way to know is to do a heart check.

Do your first thoughts bring fear and anxiety? Or do you have a sense of excitement? Our hearts will tell us where we've put our trust. The offspring of fear is hopelessness. Hebrews 6:19 says, "*Hope anchors the soul*" (emphasis added). Our soul, collectively, is our mind, will, and emotions. Hope is what faith hangs onto until it manifests. It is like the *title deed* of what we are promised (Hebrews 11:1).

Whether we face tragedy or triumphs, what our soul is anchored in is revealed to us. Will we panic, become prideful and indignant, or do we humbly submit? Do we spout off or pray? We are sometimes surprised by our reaction to a sudden storm because we had worked hard to *sanctify ourselves* (become fully set apart) in a certain area. Those reactions are just God's way of revealing how deeply rooted those emotions were that surfaced.

The areas we think least about praying for are often where our natural strength or wisdom lies usually. When we see the obvious, we might subconsciously think, I got this—easy peasy lemon squeezy! I mean, how hard is it to pump gas or go to the grocery store? It seems logical to just go through the day and make some decisions on our own. The *situation* may be simple, however, our heart may have an issue. Maybe it's not as much the situation but our disregard for God and His wisdom and not seeing everything we do as an opportunity to be an ambassador from Heaven.

It is His Word that prunes and cleanses us. There is no divide between what is natural and supernatural, so we no longer operate as ordinary men (1 Corinthians 3:3 AMP). The most minute things we do take on a significance when we do them as unto the Lord in partnership with Holy Spirit.

I will never believe God brings harm or sickness to teach us a lesson. He's not a child abuser. But, He may *use* circumstances to reveal our hearts so we can die to our old nature and allow Him to establish the born again nature and His kingdom within us, so our lives become living testimonies. Sometimes He takes us through the storms, and sometimes, He shows us the way around them. Either way, He wants us to be intimately aware He's present!

So, let's pray God would reveal our hearts. Let's not be the ones who put our trust in our own strength and wisdom but who trust in the heart of our Father. Let's ask Him to show us those things which weigh us down mentally and spiritually. Then, we can run our race with hopeful expectation, without distractions, offenses, and stumbling blocks and have a hopeful New Year!

GRAB YOUR JOURNAL!

What is God showing you at this moment?

In light of this revelation, how does this shift your thoughts and actions?

Hard Truth Wrapped in Love

READ

Hebrews 4:12,

Proverbs 18:19,

James 4:1-12,

Mark 4:14-20,

Psalms 51:6,

Proverbs 15:1-7,

Psalms 81:10

If you've ever had the pleasure of owning a dog, you know the struggle of getting them to take a pill. Tucker, our poodle (God rest his soul), put up a good fight, finding the pill in whatever we hid it in except peanut butter! He couldn't understand the medicine was to keep his heart safe from parasites, but the yumminess it was wrapped in helped it go down more easily.

Truth, like a knife, can be painful. God's Word is described as, "... sharper than any two-edged sword, penetrating as far as the division of the soul and spirit [the completeness of a person], and of both joints and marrow [the deepest parts of our nature], exposing and judging the very thoughts and intentions of the heart" (Hebrews 4:12 AMP).

A true disciple who seeks God's Word with a desire for answers and growth doesn't fear hard truths. When Holy Spirit convicts us on a heart issue, He creates both the conviction and the empowerment to change our thinking. He asks us to trust Him enough to cut into us to reveal and remove cancerous thoughts and detrimental blindness which keep us bound. A disciple willingly submits to His sword, understanding His love and acceptance, desiring His best, knowing it leads to peace and freedom.

However, it is difficult for non-believers to swallow tough truths. They don't know how to trust a God who demands they lay down all they've built their lives on. It doesn't sound pleasant. How easy it is to throw our opinions of these truths around to friends, family, or social media, but doing so can make us *seem* crass and judgmental? If our words are not *tempered with love*, we overwhelm people with words that crush the spirit (Proverbs 15:4, my paraphrase).

On the other hand, we can't be afraid to bring conviction which might offend.

Jesus Himself often upset people. But, He never pointed at their sin (except for the Pharisees who misrepresented God) and neither should we. Instead, Jesus focused on removing the mental and spiritual parasites that kept them separated from His love and grace. If our intent is to love people, we'll build relationships and trust, becoming a living sacrifice. Patiently, we will water, plant seeds of life instead of forcing a harvest, offending and hardening the hearts of the very people God is pursuing. Proverbs 18:19 (TPT) says, "It is easier to conquer a strong city than to win back a friend whom you've offended. Their walls go up, making it nearly impossible to win them back." We must come to them with hard truths wrapped in love, just as a Tucker's pills were wrapped in peanut butter.

We need the Holy Spirit to give us wisdom and guide us in how to do this. When people see we genuinely love them and are not trying to sell them something, they're more apt to open up. Proverbs 27:6 (GNT) tells us, "Friends mean well, even when they hurt you. But when an enemy puts his arm around your shoulder—watch out!"

People are not our enemy, and we cannot allow our *own* hearts to become frustrated with those who are blind to truth. Rather than accusing the blind of not seeing, let's offer them a hand and lead them to the One who can help them see.

Before spouting off our convictions, let's check to see if our desire is more than simple behavior modification that eases frustration with their habits. Let us only speak if our desire is to bring them into a relationship with Christ. Let's guard our hearts against attitudes that fuel contention and ask God how to respond so when we open our mouths, He will fill it! (Psalms 81:10)

GRAB YOUR JOURNAL!

What is God showing you at this moment?

In light of this revelation, how does this shift your thoughts and actions?

Handling Heart Questions

READ

Job 1:1,

Proverbs 4:23,

1 Samuel 16:6-8,

John 9:1-3,

Ephesians 3,

Hebrews 6:19,

Ephesians 3:16-21

I was talking with a friend who is going through an intense trial. Her family has endured more in the last few years than anyone could imagine, brought on by no fault of their own. My heart breaks for what they have dealt with 24 hours a day for the last several years. My friend made a statement to me once that I still pray through, talking in love of her now disabled, adopted son, "He doesn't deserve to have to go through this," as she and her family still stand strong and exhausted because they *have to*. There *is* no retreat in this battle. Like Job, their son is blameless and upright. He is righteous and honors God even in his condition. It's hard to understand his stamina and faith.

So, I write this with trepidation because I never want to appear as if I have it all together. This devotional is not about my friend, but in prayer, sorting through the struggle with the same questions.

It's natural to look at situations and judge them as either deserving or undeserving. We become angry when the wicked prosper or the righteous go through trials. Our desire for an answer becomes our grid of right and wrong. When trials come, the root of bitterness can go straight to our hearts, and we may wind up judging God by our hurt. Above all things, we must guard our hearts!

In the culture of Jesus' day, people who were afflicted were considered to have brought a curse upon themselves. Jesus threw that argument out when he healed the man born blind saying there had been no sin (See John 9:3). But in the same way, we don't sin our way into sickness, we don't grace ourselves into healing. We don't earn God's favor, and the attempt to do so is called "self-righteous."

Satan is known as the *accuser* (Revelation 12:10), and he accuses us before

God but also accuses God to us, causing us to judge by appearance, which only causes feelings of doubt and separation from God and each other. The Devil searches for weaknesses to bring offense, disconnecting us from our Power Source and diminishing our effectiveness for His kingdom. Not that we don't *do* good works, but now, our works are the focus, instead of power in Holy Spirit. Our heart is unplugged from Holy Spirit before we are fully charged. We try to do in our own power what only He can do in us or through us.

Weeds in our hearts must be choked out by intense love, which can only be found in the presence of God. Ephesians 3 says it best. We must be rooted and grounded, strengthened in our innermost being by the power of the Holy Spirit to know the intimate depth, width, breadth, and height of the love of Christ. Hebrews 6:19 (NIV) says we have "this hope as an anchor for the soul." If our eyes are on *anything* other than His love for us, we become disconnected.

I continually remind myself to stay plugged in, turned on, and tuned in to His love, and His love alone. Nothing else matters. I must be rooted and grounded in Love, for He is my strength. I cannot afford to be sidetracked by the Enemy's devices. I cannot do this by myself. But, I am not alone. My Father has an endless supply, and He loves me.

GRAB YOUR JOURNAL!

What is God showing you at this moment?

In light of this revelation, how does this shift your thoughts and actions?

How Much Do You Want to Spend?

READ
Matthew 6:19-21,
Proverbs 13:22,
Romans 4,
Philippians 4:6-19,
Matthew 6:5-6

I jokingly say the reason I can't hold a grudge is because I have a terrible memory. But, in all honesty, I just can't afford to. It costs more than I want to pay—spiritually, physically, and emotionally. I refuse to "spend" huge amounts of time on useless emotional turmoil which steals from and corrupts my heart, costing me my peace and joy. The price is too great!

Matthew 6:19-21 refers to a kind of a bank account in Heaven where treasure can be stored. It also says not to store up treasure here on Earth which can be consumed or stolen. Not that we shouldn't save or leave an inheritance to our kids, but I think He has a deeper meaning here.

What if love was our currency? What if we actually spent time instead of money? What if our quality of life or the ones we hold dearest depended on the wealth of our hearts' attitudes, pride, and desires? What if how we spent our day was reflected in our Heavenly account?

There are people we refer to as *spiritually bankrupt*. We know those who are *rich in love*. Romans 4:3 says Abraham believed in God, and it was *"credited to his account"* as righteousness. When we are in the midst of a constant daily struggle, we are often spent at the end of each day.

That's why it's so important to go before our Father who has an endless supply. His throne is where we deposit our cares and receive all we need before returning to the fight. (If we don't come away encouraged and strengthened, we may be complaining instead of praying).

How could the apostle Paul rejoice in prison, in beatings, in near-death experiences? His account was full, and he was free, *even in prison*! This life is impossible without Christ, but with Him, *all things* are possible (Philippians 4:13)! His presence and wisdom are required for us to maneuver victoriously through the impossible. We cannot do Christ-life without Him. However, *His supply* is limitless (Philippians 4:19), and we, like Paul, must learn to draw on our eternal account!

Is it possible to forgive those who've hurt us? Just how important is it for us to hold onto an offense at the cost of peace? Do we hold our sense of justice in higher esteem than Christ in us? Let's fill our account by trusting God in the hard places, spending our time loving, and investing in love. His precious resources are something we can bank on.

GRAB YOUR JOURNAL!

What is God showing you at this moment?

In light of this revelation, how does this shift your thoughts and actions?

What Did I Just Step Into?

READ

Luke 14:26-33,

1 Corinthians 3:3,

Ephesians 3:1-21,

1 Chronicles 4:10,

Mark 16:20,

1 Corinthians 2:16,

Romans 12:1-2,

Romans 8:6-15,

Galatians 2:20,

2 Corinthians 4:3-4,

Mark 16:17-18,

John 18:36,

John 17:9-26,

Galatians 5:6

Very seldom do we ever approach a new career, life chapter, or new task, fully aware of what it will require of us. How many times have we said, "If I had known it was going to be like this, I would have..." We had no idea of the commitment or how we would have to rearrange schedules, adjust our families, and our way of life to accommodate what we had just stepped into. Of course, we should always count the costs before diving into any new venture, and if the potential reward outweighs the risks, but we will never fully understand it until we're neck deep in the middle of it.

When we were first born again, many of us were simply looking for peace, a Father, unconditional love, or escape from eternal damnation. We may have been raised in a Christian home, and it was just "the logical thing to do." But, until we begin to delve into our Christian walk in beloved sonship, we don't fully understand what it means to *live born again*.

It entails leaving behind a dead past and *mere mortal* ways of life (1 Corinthians 3:3). It means learning to lean into our faith in a loving Father who wants to prosper us in more ways than we can imagine (Ephesians 3:20). It means learning how to be not only a son of God but His ambassador on assignment; enlisting our Father, the King, to change our areas of influence in our job, family, and community. It means leaving behind old ways of thinking, understanding that being born *again* means not only a new identity but actually *thinking* like God.

Kingdom-minded doesn't mean *doing* in our own strength *for* God but doing things *through Christ, God's way*. We are never to approach a situation without knowing that He is *in us* and wants to show Himself *through* us. We will know our mind is becoming renewed to His way of thinking when we are not intimidated by the impossible. We'll begin to look for ways that God can manifest Himself through us in miracles, signs, and wonders. We won't want to sit in front of a TV when we can pray for people in Walmart and have them healed, saved, and delivered! We won't be intimidated by a world which wants us to shut up and keep this gospel hidden because they have blinders on which have kept them from seeing Christ as Love (2 Corinthians 4:3-4)!

We are not orphans who are begging. We are children of the Most High God, learning to navigate a kingdom without being led by our senses (Romans 8:6-15). Our faith only works through love. Let's renew our minds so He establishes His kingdom in us, around us, and through us, as we begin to see ourselves as citizens of Heaven on assignment for our King (John 17:16).

GRAB YOUR JOURNAL!

What is God showing you at this moment?

In light of this revelation, how does this shift your thoughts and actions?

Servants, Sons, and Friends

READ

John 15:7-15,

John 6:2,

1 John 4:1-21,

2 Corinthians 9:6-8,

James 2:14-18,

Proverbs 19:17,

Galatians 5:5-7

One of my coworkers had a proud mommy moment in her daughter's newfound maturity. She is so proud of the change in her daughter now that she has started college and is working part-time. Her daughter attends school close by, so she is able to live at home. She is beginning to see things around the house which need to be done and does them without being asked like putting gas in her mom's car. When she is asked to help out, she no longer gives the old 'teenage eye-roll.' The smile on this mama's face couldn't be bought!

When we were kids, we did things because our parents "said so." We didn't know why we had to make our beds or clean our room. It was a slavish chore in our eyes (John 15:15). As we got a little older, we did things out of respect or obligation. Our vision became clearer, and we realized how hard our parents worked. We didn't care why we had to do them, we just knew it was the right thing to do (Ephesians 6:2). But, when we came to experience the Love of Christ, we began to do things out of our relationship with Holy Spirit. When His love flows out of us toward the people in our circle of influence, whether our family, friends, co-workers, or someone in need, it is revelatory love that comes through friendship with God (2 Corinthians 9:7).

The more our revelation of God's love for us, the easier it is for us to love others. 1 John 4:7-8 (TPT, emphasis added) says, "Those who are loved by God, let his love continually pour from you to one another, because God is love. Everyone who loves is *fathered by God* and experiences an *intimate knowledge of him*. The one who doesn't love has yet to *know* God, for God is love."

If we're struggling with loving people, fulfilling obligations, or acting in obedience to God, we simply don't know Him *in that area*. If our faith fails, it may be because we are filtering what God wants us to do through wounded minds and spirits, allowing the past to dictate our actions toward people.

Like a curtain on a rod, faith hangs on love (Galatians 5:5-7). Without love, faith falls flat. And, we can't *truly* love without real relationship. If we are shrouded in doubt and suspicion of God, our faith is lacking. If faith is lacking, it's because we are *ignorant* of our Supplier.

If we're *doing* because of compulsion, let's tweak our attitude by exercising our spirit, infusing ourselves with love, so our actions aren't begrudging or obligatory. If a homeless person approaches us, let's refrain from judgment, but rather pray for and bless him by our revelation of grace (James 2:16), knowing God is a debtor to no man, and he that lends to the poor, lends to the Lord (Proverbs 19:17).

As we begin to stretch our faith in God's covenant with us, let's lean a little closer to His chest to hear His heartbeat and meditate on His love for us until we are secure in our friendship with Him as dear friends. If we abide (fully and completely) in Him, and His Word abides (fully and completely) in us, we shall ask what we will, and it shall be done for us of our Father in Heaven (John 15:7).

GRAB YOUR JOURNAL! | *What is God showing you at this moment?*

In light of this revelation, how does this shift your thoughts and actions?

Secondhand Lions

READ

John 14:1,

John 14:12-27,

Mark 9:23,

Mark 11:23-25,

John 5:39-44,

Galatians 6:9,

John 17:25-26,

1 Corinthians 13:11-13

One of my favorite movies is *Secondhand Lions*. It's about a timid young boy whose irresponsible mother leaves him with two wealthy, but grumpy, great-uncles who have hoarded their riches. Over the course of the summer, they come to know each other and his Uncle Garth regales him with amazing adventures of their past lives; of sultans and princesses, battles and treasures! Those adventurous stories seem like tall tales until they are challenged by their mother's greedy boyfriend who wants to know where the money is hidden. The boyfriend lies to young Walter about how the money was stolen and that the uncles were bank-robbing fugitives.

Walter is faced with a choice to either believe the far-fetched stories of his uncles or one which seems more logical. But because of the bond he has built with these two old men, he heroically chooses to believe in his uncles.

These amazing stories stirred his courage to become like these two old men he'd come to love and respect. But it wasn't until he was grown, he found out all of the stories he had been told were indeed true.

Over and over, we are challenged to take what God says as truth. We are faced with impossible situations and seemingly impossible people time and again. We may have a background of mistrust because of past hurts, betrayals, or failures because we've been shaped by the world. Yet, we read these amazing stories in the Bible, of kings and battles, and treasures which cause our hearts to soar with *hope*! His Word beckons and challenges us, *"only believe."*

As we find ourselves becoming more intimate with God, we begin seeing ourselves differently. We identify with different circumstances and people in the

Bible. Our character takes shape and boldness begins to sprout from seed form.

When our belief system is fueled by relationship in our passionate pursuit of God, our identity becomes that of a beloved child, instead of an abandoned orphan. When we respond as a trusted friend, rather than a hired hand, we begin to believe the impossible is not only *possible* but *part of our purpose*.

This kind of pursuit in relationship with Holy Spirit can't be built in a one hour a week corporate gathering. It must trump social media, television, and hobbies, and should affect our earthly relationships. Our primary focus isn't merely *information*, to prove how much we know, but *transformation*, becoming personified love.

Relationship is constant fellowship and flow of conversation, plans, and vulnerability. It's a transfer of hearts between two parties, and the goal is intimacy. We make a choice to believe by faith, and the exclamation point at the end of our journey will be when we see Him face to face in Heaven and everything we've built our lives on becomes visible!

Let's really know our Father, so the love with which God and Jesus have for each other and for us may be in us, overwhelming our hearts, giving us the courage to believe! Let's purify our motives, set ourselves to seek Him, and find what our hearts have been searching for, so when the world's logic tugs at us, we won't be shaken nor moved!

GRAB YOUR JOURNAL! | *What is God showing you at this moment?*

In light of this revelation, how does this shift your thoughts and actions?

Letting God Judge Your Heart

READ

Genesis 3:1-7,

Hebrews 4:12,

Matthew 16:24-27,

Ephesians 2,

Romans 6:1-6,

Hebrews 11:6

"Only God Can Judge Me," is a slogan I've seen on t-shirts, and my best guess is it refers to a song entitled the same by a rap artist who died violently several years ago. Getting my religious mind past the colorful metaphors he used in the lyrics, I found my heart burdened for his soul, seemingly searching for peace, knowing somehow it had to be in God, but life had twisted it under the influence of Satan. It seemed he lived, trying to satisfy the hunger in his spirit by feeding on things that could only satisfy his flesh, ultimately leading to his death.

As Christians, we are not to live by the fear of man, nor the opinion of popular culture, but we also are not to live by the dictates of our own flesh. Ephesians 2 says *now* that we are in Christ, we are not to follow the way of this world, under the sway of the present age, like we were before. We resist partnering with demonic spirits, through carelessness, rebellion, or unbelieving because it goes against the purposes of God.

Even though we believe in Jesus and His work on the cross, is it possible to maintain and even cultivate rebellion inwardly while doing all the religious rituals or good deeds we think are going to get us into Heaven? If we are trying to make God fit into our thinking by twisting a scripture here and there to fit our lifestyle, our own spirit has already judged us as rebellious (Hebrews. 4:12). If deep down, we say, "I know what God's Word says, but…" we are falling for the same deception Satan used against Eve in Genesis 3.

I'm not just talking about what we consider the *big* sins. We probably won't be tempted to rob a bank or murder someone today, but what about worry which robs us of peace? What about the unbelief creeping in as we've had to stand in faith for years? What about unforgiveness which holds someone accountable to the point we lose sight of who God created them to be? What about the anger towards our kids and family keeping us from representing Christ to them? What about those attitudes toward the church where we may have been hurt in the past?

God has already judged the born-again believer as righteous, but He has also judged those attitudes as *unfit for His children*. So, we must die to those lesser things to find real life in Christ. It's not through works and striving but in yielding and trusting (which to many of us is harder than striving and working).

We will never truly know the Light until we choose to walk in Him, learning to receive empowering grace through faith through the growing process of submitting and trusting our hearts to Holy Spirit.

GRAB YOUR JOURNAL!

What is God showing you at this moment?

In light of this revelation, how does this shift your thoughts and actions?

Just How Sure is Your Foundation?

READ

John 14:26-27,
Hebrews 4:10-16,
Proverbs 3:5-8,
Matthew 6:34,
John 16:33,
Ephesians 6:10-19,
Isaiah 33:6

I found myself precariously perched on a step-ladder, painting the crown molding over the bathtub. Too lazy to move the ladder one more time, I leaned in as far as I could, lightly placing my foot on the handle of the sliding shower door which was loose from the bottom track. It swung with me as I stretched over to put on the finishing touch. It was not a safe move, but my weariness was speaking louder than my common sense. No matter how unstable, I just needed a place to rest my foot in order to *feel* like I wouldn't fall. Disaster was averted, but the story could have easily gone the other way.

We do this a lot in our thought-life. We keep on searching for a *why* for issues that *have none*, except the Devil is a jerk, and we live in a fallen world. We create doctrines to comfort ourselves when our answers are delayed. We blame others, thinking they didn't have enough faith when they are not instantly healed. We think things like "God needed another angel" when someone passes unexpectedly. We want something to lean into, no matter how weak or unstable, which seems logical, but like a loose shower door not meant to hold my weight, it can give way, and we'll come crashing down.

My heart cries for the things around me; the political, social, and racial unrest; a child leaving earth; a tired friend with a seemingly incurable sick child, whose faith is waning as they wonder where God is; and righteous friends battling cancer. Feeling the screws tighten on my heart until I know it's about to explode, I hear, "Guard your heart," whispered over and over again in my spirit. God is reminding me not to base my faith in my lack of seeing and understanding as I once again struggle to enter into His rest (Hebrews 4:10-11).

If Jesus is the *absolute Lord* in my life, there are times when I don't have to understand. I put my trust in Him and follow without question. There may be times I must wait for revelation or answers, but if I try to come up with my own, I'm keeping God out of the equation and satisfying myself with my best guess. We gave up the throne, gave up the right to know when we *gave ourselves* to Christ.

Let's start with what we do know. God is not a thief. The Devil comes to steal, kill, and destroy (John 10:10). The Devil is the ruler of the principalities around us (Ephesians 6:12), and his goal is to do enough harm for us to lose faith, blame God, and become ineffective as world changers.

Ephesians 6:17 (TPT) says, "Embrace the power of salvation's full deliverance, like a helmet *to protect your thoughts from lies*." As Christians, we are called to *lean into* the faith that is greater than our understanding, accepting its strength and protection. It may be uncomfortable as we shift from feelings to faith, but He is the *sure foundation*. I like the way senior pastor of Bethel Church Bill Johnson said it, "We have the *honor* of standing in a mystery, not empowering the questions of 'why' and 'how long'—having done *all*, to *still stand*, when there is no breakthrough, and still have the *'yes'* to our Lord, in our heart."

GRAB YOUR JOURNAL!

What is God showing you at this moment?

In light of this revelation, how does this shift your thoughts and actions?

King of the Jungle

READ

2 Corinthians 10:3-6,

Ephesians 6:10-18,

1 John 4:1,

Mark 4:24 (TPT),

Mark 9:20-26 (NIV),

Proverbs 4:23 (TPT),

1 Peter 1:13,

Romans 12:1-2,

Philippians 4:6-7,

1 Peter 5:7,

Matthew 11:28-30,

Psalms 55:22,

Psalms 23:4,

Psalms 56:3

Have you ever noticed odd behaviors and wondered how a person could ever arrive at the conclusion that what they were doing was logical?

Watching an episode of *Hoarders*, I saw a seemingly normal person in every other sense, living in rat-infested filth. But there are also less dramatic examples. I know of a shy introvert who exhibits intense anxiety and anger in traffic. Some may develop odd behaviors, habits, or phobias because of trauma. I know soldiers who have returned from combat, who feel they must position themselves in a room, even in safe places, to see everyone coming and going. I know young people who have experienced some form of trauma, rejection, or thought-process, while their identity is still immature, which has made them question their sexuality, humanity, or purpose in life.

What offends our spirit in one aspect of life can have a profound influence on how we make decisions in others. Seedling thoughts take root and fester into habits or actions which shape our lives. Sometimes it may take professional help or a revelation from God to deconstruct the lies we've told ourselves.

Since I hear from God through mental pictures most of the time, I see in my mind's eye a child falling from a tree branch then swinging from vine to vine. Tiring from endless swinging, he searches for the next landing. Not caring if the next branch is rotten or home to a snake, he will take any respite from weariness.

When hurt, anger, or fear hits us, we often fall like that child from the tree branch. Our minds grab hold of the first logical "thought vine" to keep us from careening out of control, then we swing from thought to thought until we find footing that feels logical or comfortable. It doesn't matter if it's built on deception as long as we can make sense of it and find momentary peace. If we don't stop ourselves, we'll have swung ourselves deep into a jungle with no easy way out.

This is why 2 Corinthians 10:5 (TPT) tells us to demolish *every* deceptive thought, judging it against God's Word, insisting it bow to the Anointed One. Ephesians 6:18 (TPT) says, "Embrace the power of salvation's full deliverance, like a helmet *to protect your thoughts from lies*." By empowering our spirit with faith and truth, we will begin to discern the spirits, by "examining what they say" (1 John 4:1 TPT).

In Mark 4:24 (TPT, emphasis added), Jesus says, *"Be diligent to understand the meaning* behind everything you hear, for as you do, *more understanding* will be given to you..."* The more we are tender to hear, the more we receive. But, it's when we insist our *feelings* are truth, however, we lose even what understanding we have. Then, we are left to navigate the jungle on our own.

God *is* love, and *apart* from love, we will be overcome by fear of the unknown. Then, we become weary, grasping, anxious Christians, pushing discomfort aside by creating our own doctrines to comfort us in darkness, never acknowledging our weakness, never submitting it to God. May we be like the man in Mark 9:24 who brought his hopelessly tormented child to Jesus, saying, "I believe, but *help me overcome my unbelief*" (NIV, emphasis added). God knows our deepest thoughts already, so we can be transparent, acknowledging pain without making it a part of our identity.

Let's stop being ruled by our thoughts, opinions, and feelings, choosing instead to hold those thoughts *accountable* to Christ by measuring them against the light of God's Word and His love. Let's be grafted into the True Vine, deeply rooted in Him, and allow Jesus to be the King of our jungle.

GRAB YOUR JOURNAL!

What is God showing you at this moment?

In light of this revelation, how does this shift your thoughts and actions?

Why We Worship

READ

Psalms 100,

1 Thessalonians 5:18,

Ephesians 2:6-10,

1 Corinthians 13:4-13,

Mark 16:17-18,

Revelation 12:10-12,

Ephesians 5:1,

Proverbs 1:7,

Proverbs 9:10, 2

Corinthians 3:2-3,

Hebrews 11:6,

1 John 3:2

Praise and worship time at my church is exceptional! God has truly gifted our worship team with excellence from the sound engineers, to dancers and flags, to the singers and musicians. There is total liberty to cut loose and dance, losing yourself in worship, attracting no attention, which is good for me because my dancing skills are about one level above the hokey pokey.

I've come to be very aware of the motives behind my worship. In my early Christian walk, there were times when my worship was needs driven, desperate for God to move because I was actively engaged. There have been times it has been battle driven, where worship was an act of faith, where I wanted all the forces of hell to know they would not win. Neither are incorrect as we are learning to give praise with thanksgiving in every situation (1 Thessalonians 5:18). The Psalms are full of worship fueled by times of celebration, depression, loss, and war.

But, the more we come to know God, the deeper the revelation of His love toward us, the more the motive behind our worship is reshaped. We enter His presence with thanksgiving and respond to His presence, His faithfulness, and goodness. There's almost a peaceful anticipation knowing whatever we may go through, what we may not understand, or how things will work out, the God of the universe desires *us*. Our lives are no longer our own! We belong to Him, and He wants *us* to be *one with Him*! How can we *not* worship Him?

Worship is not for God's benefit. It's not something God *needs* from us but something He is worthy of. *He is love*, and He is complete in and of Himself. While we are pouring out our devotion to Him, love is fully focused on the target at which He is aimed—us! He knows we become *like* what we worship. As we worship Him as our main desire and focus, He invades our lives and rewards us with Himself, so our lives witness to the world around us (Hebrews 11:6, 2 Corinthians 3:2-3). Worship causes us to sit with Him in Heavenly places (Ephesians 2:6) and see from His point of view. We move from a place of serving Him out of duty, to partnering with Him as His children.

We begin to see the enemy under our feet, to love without fear, and preach with signs following. Our lives and blessings become secondary as we are filled to overflowing with acceptance from our perfect Father. So, cut loose in worship and rejoice *freely* in the knowledge of Him, *as we become like Him* (John 3:2)!

GRAB YOUR JOURNAL!

What is God showing you at this moment?

In light of this revelation, how does this shift your thoughts and actions?

Let Me Shed Some Light on that For You

READ

2 Corinthians 5:17,

Colossians 1:12-14,

Ephesians 5:8-14,

1 John 1:6-8,

Matthew 13:12-16,

Proverbs 4:18,

Matthew 6:9-13

There's an old saying I grew up hearing, "Le'me shed some light on that for ya." In a courtroom, one might more properly say, "In light of new evidence, we find the defendant..." Colossians 1:12 says *we've been transferred out of darkness*. We are now in the *kingdom of light*. But, we were used to the darkness and moved in it somewhat successfully. Even as Christians, we may yet revert to our old thinking out of habit, never realizing we left God out of the equation.

Learning to walk in His light takes practice, often includes failure, but is designed for our transformation, and it starts with God's Word. Even our ideas of success must change. Where we may see praying for someone who doesn't receive their healing right away as our failure, God sees a child exercising and perfecting their faith.

When we are born again by Christ Jesus, we are taken out of one kingdom and placed in another. We used to walk in darkness, but now, we walk in the light. Even though our spirit is instantly pure, our minds must be renewed, because our views and opinions *which used to be made apart from God*, are *now partnering with Holy Spirit* for His divine purpose.

Light allows us to walk freely without fear of running into obstacles. He also shows us thought patterns we live by which are contrary to His Word. We must *learn* to walk in His light. We must *transform our thinking* as an ambassador from another world. We cannot even *begin* to understand this light until we are born *again* (John 1:5), and even then, the transformation process is just that: an *eternal process*. As we walk in *all the light we know*, we will be given more and more (Proverbs 4:18 and Matthew 13:12).

Let's begin transforming our minds by seeing God as a perfect and loving Father (Matthew 6:9). When we see ourselves as His dear children, we see ourselves in the "family business" of transforming the world to look like Heaven (Matthew 6:10).

Once He sheds His light on *whose* we are and *who* we are, we'll give up the right to start any problem with our lack of resources (Matthew 6:11). We'll then be able to see and love others as Christ loved us (Matthew 6:12). Seeing all He has done to adopt us in His eternal Kingdom, let's willingly and enthusiastically die to our selfish nature, so we are not tempted. Then, as we grow to love Him more, His nature will become our nature and He will be glorified through our lives!

GRAB YOUR JOURNAL!

What is God showing you at this moment?

In light of this revelation, how does this shift your thoughts and actions?

To Me, Then Through Me

READ

Hebrews 5:12,

Matthew 6:33,

3 John 4,

1 Corinthians 3:1-3,

Luke 2:52,

Ephesians 2:10 (TPT),

1 Corinthians 12:4-27,

Romans 12:1-13,

1 Corinthians 13:11,

Philippians 4:13

If you've ever watched a toddler for any length of time, it's highly entertaining. They are just one big, wobbly giggle, finding hilarity in the silly noises we make for them. They start mimicking their parents' behaviors, enjoying the same interests or sense of humor. But, their lack of coordination and maturity makes them completely needs-driven. Any time they are hurt, hungry, or uncomfortable, they cry for mom or dad to fix, feed, or meet the need. As parents, it is our *joy* to fulfill it.

But, we would be remiss as parents if our grown children still ran to us to bandage a skinned knee. Parents who model God's nature teach children to navigate life, make decisions, and set things right. So it is in the kingdom. As young believers are just beginning to learn to navigate newfound faith, it's fine to run to "Dad" for every little thing. But, as we mature and grow in faith, we are to partner with Father, allowing Him to do *through* us instead of *for* us quite so much. If we are under-developed for our age, it should be a flashing warning light to us.

Matthew 6:33 (NKJV) says, "Seek first the kingdom of God..." That means we set our heart and submit our will to display God's dominion in every area of our lives. The second part of the verse, "and His righteousness" is His way of doing and being right. It's having the attitude and character of God. The last part of the scripture, "and all these things shall be added to you," is a result of the first. Often, we make the "all these things" our primary focus of prayer, and forget the first half of the command.

While it is true that we rely on God in everything, it is also true that He desires to show Himself through us. Instead of simply praying for God to provide a miracle, He desires for our intercession so miracles can come through the authority given to us as kings and priests on behalf of others in our sphere of influence, hopefully instilling the same passion for a relationship with Holy Spirit in them!

It is God's joy to manifest Himself to us. But, it is a greater joy to Him for us to co-labor with Him (3 John 4). Let us honor our Father, by seeking first to be like Him, allowing Him to manifest His presence not only to us but through us, as light to a dark world.

GRAB YOUR JOURNAL! | *What is God showing you at this moment?*

In light of this revelation, how does this shift your thoughts and actions?

Finding the Joy

READ
John 16:33,
John 10:10,
James 1:2-8,
Romans 5:17,
Hebrews 5:7-9,
Romans 8:2-4,
2 Corinthians 4:8-10,
Matthew 5:8-16,
1 Corinthians 13:7,
Galatians 5:16-26

I don't know about you, but I do not enjoy trials and tribulations. There is nothing enjoyable about persecution. So, why do many of our God-given assignments include: walk through valleys, overcome, fear not, cast worries, maintain faith, endure all things, and find joy in trials? (Ain't *none* of that *any* fun!)

Let me start by saying, God doesn't bring destruction to test us, rather, He wants us equipped for when it comes, as it surely will.

James 1 says the greatest opportunity to experience joy is found when our faith is tested because it stirs up power to endure all things, producing endurance, releasing perfection to every part of our being until there is nothing lacking or missing (James 1:2-3 TPT).

Oh, that we would courageously walk through fire for someone else's salvation, that we would willingly take their scorn to allow them to see how much God loves them! May we be so mission-minded that injustice towards us would have no negative effect on our walk of faith and grace, but that we would rule in life, like Christ!

Jesus learned obedience through the things he suffered (Hebrews 5:8). As a devoted son, He was fully submitted to His Father's will. He suffered persecution for His convictions and for those for whom He had compassion. He learned to listen closely to His Father for wisdom and instruction because of His focus on the eternal rather than the temporal. His kind of love is, "in your face," and calls us to go deeper. When we love deeply, things may get messy. We are naturally going to be touched by the conditions of others.

Yet, while we are in this world, we are not of it. As citizens of Heaven, we are ambassadors to a world which is not our home. We live by laws that supersede the laws of this earthly kingdom. We have access to certain diplomatic immunities that keep us free from the law of sin and death. 2 Corinthians 4:8-10 (TPT) says,"Though we experience every kind of pressure, we're not crushed. At times we don't know what to do, but quitting is not an option. We are persecuted by others, but God has not forsaken us. We may be knocked down, but not out. We continually share in the death of Jesus in our own bodies so that the resurrection life of Jesus will be revealed through our humanity."

British evangelist and pioneer of the pentecostal revival in the early 20th century, Smith Wigglesworth, said it best: "God wants to purify our minds until we can bear all things, believe all things, hope all things and endure all things. God dwells in you, but you cannot have this divine power until you live and walk in the Holy Ghost, until the power of the new life is greater than the old life."

We are God's beloved children, so let's pray whatever trial may come our way, our Father is revealed to those around us as we stand on His eternal promises that He never leaves us nor forsakes us, that He gives us wisdom and power to overcome.

GRAB YOUR JOURNAL!

What is God showing you at this moment?

In light of this revelation, how does this shift your thoughts and actions?

Bride vs. Concubine

READ
John 6:32-69,
Philippians 4:11-13,
Philippians 4:17-19,
Acts 17:28,
Ephesians 5:25-27,
Revelation 19:7-9,
Revelation 21:2,
Revelation 21:9,
James 1:2-8,
John 6:53

Growing up in the 80's, I saw a lot of people drawn to church because of what was being taught. The thought of God "blessing" us and meeting "all of our needs" was like a fisherman chumming the waters for game fish. Many people came for those reasons. I'm not saying God doesn't bless and meet needs, but the motive by which they were drawn left a lot of people disillusioned and disappointed. Gifts were sought at the expense of the Giver, so when the wishing well didn't produce the way it was supposed to, many left the church and blamed God, or stayed in a place of constantly failing to live up to a standard to obtain favor from God to create an explanation for their lack of blessing.

They didn't understand God's desire for relationship is that of a bride, not a concubine.

In Biblical times, concubines were taken by a king simply for his pleasure, as a measure of wealth. So many Christians seem to act like concubines instead of brides, who dutifully wait to be called into the bedchamber for an occasional touch. She is task-oriented for the hope of favor. When she leaves, she simply waits for the next touch. Whereas a bride has full access to the inner chamber—the secret place—and can create the atmosphere for intimacy. She *knows* her husband and knows wherever she is, she carries his name, his presence, his authority. She knows she can place her trust in him even if she doesn't always understand him.

Christ is coming for his bride, the church (Ephesians 5:27). Circumstances and trials are good ways to get a bearing on that identity. Do we get our "Sunday fix" and hope whatever the pastor says gives us Holy Ghost goosebumps? Are we counting it all joy when we fall into diverse temptations, trusting He is making a way to glorify His name through us? Are we willing to walk through the dark places and shine His light, or just rehearse and reiterate the problems, while putting our faith in the strength of mere men? Are we waiting on God to move, or are we *moving with Him,* having become one with Him to complete His purpose?

Tests will challenge our identity. Once, Jesus tested the crowd which followed Him simply because He performed miracles. So, when He said in John 6:53, "unless you eat the flesh of the Son of Man and drink his blood, you have no life in you," (John 6:53 NIV) it offended their natural mind, yet Jesus didn't bother giving them a sermon on what He meant. Those who stuck around for the healing and food were unwilling to get past the offense to gain revelation, and many of his disciples left Him. Only the twelve knew, even though they didn't understand everything, His words had life!

God is building an unshakable kingdom which goes far beyond our thoughts and experiences. We are a part of His plan. We know He is the Way, Truth, and Life, so we are left with the choice. Will we *settle* for the life of a concubine or *be* the bride of Christ He intended for us to be?

GRAB YOUR JOURNAL!

What is God showing you at this moment?

In light of this revelation, how does this shift your thoughts and actions?

In Over Our Heads

READ

Luke 17:5-10,

John 3:16-17,

Psalms 28:6-9,

Deuteronomy 31:6,

1 Corinthians 10:13,

Mark 10:27-31,

Mark 8:33-35,

John 14:15-17

A few weeks ago, I began praying for God to increase my faith, to take me deeper in Him. Sounds like a noble and sweet prayer. But, Holy Spirit said something to me which made me stop and think, *Do you really want more faith? You really want to walk closer to Me?*

I thought this was a no-brainer. What Christian doesn't want to walk closer and have more faith?

"Do you know what you're asking Me to do? You're asking Me to take you places where you can't rely on your own wisdom. You're asking me to remove the safety nets. You're asking Me to take you in over your head. Are you sure you want this?"

I would love to brag and say I gave Him a resounding yes, but truthfully, I'm having to answer on a moment by moment basis.

Every day, I'm presented with opportunities where I keep my mouth shut when He would have me speak and vice versa. Every day, I'm offered the chance to pray for or pass by total strangers who need His touch. Every day, He gives me a choice to *represent* Him or put a basket over my head.

If we are sincere in our prayer for increased faith, Holy Spirit will show us things through His eyes. He will begin to make us more sensitive to the needs of others, in the midst of dealing with our own messes. In Hillsong United's sweet poetic song, "Oceans," the prayer is we'll be in waters so deep He's the only thing we can trust. It sounds so enchanting, but it's a prayer to sink or walk on water. It's that comfortably uncomfortable feeling we get when we're about to move away from the normal into the new. Our "fight or flight" response kicks into high gear. In the blink of an eye, we get to decide if we're going to go our own way or step wholeheartedly into the adventure of the *impossible without Him*. It may not always be fun or easy, but never boring! Once we dive in and get over the shock, we know we are bringing our Father to a situation that needs Him, sometimes at our expense. We are to be involved and active in the process, becoming more like *Him*; the *One* who gave Himself for us!

He has given us Holy Spirit because He *knew* we'd be in various situations which would require a Helper, Comforter, Advocate, Intercessor, Counselor, Strengthener, and Standby.

Let's make a consistent daily decision to follow Him, either walking on water or in over our heads, willing to be *comfortably uncomfortable*, comforted by the Comforter.

GRAB YOUR JOURNAL!

What is God showing you at this moment?

In light of this revelation, how does this shift your thoughts and actions?

Give Me Some of That!

READ

Romans 4:18-21,

Hebrews 5:11-13,

1 Corinthians 3,

Psalms 34:8-11,

Matthew 13:10-30,

Hebrews 4:11-16,

Proverbs 16:9,

2 Corinthians 3:2-3

Have you ever stared at the menu of a new restaurant with absolutely no idea what to order? Then a waiter walks by with a plate that looks divine and sets it on the table of someone near you. You have no idea what it is, but the sight and aroma makes your mouth water, and you tell your waiter, "I'll have what he's having!"

But, what if instead of ordering, we simply sat there watching the person enjoy his meal? First, that would just be weird, but secondly, we would only be spectators of what is available to us! Certainly, he could tell us how it tastes, but he'd be the only one getting full! Why cheat ourselves out of the experience, especially when someone else has already paid for it?

Yet, many of us have this exact notion when we go to church. We may get into praise and worship a little, then sit, waiting for the pastor to share the Word about what God has done and how good He is. No matter *how awesome* the sermon, it isn't going to be enough to strengthen us through the week.

Hebrews 5:11-14 says the people are in need of milk because they are infants, doctrinally inexperienced in the word of righteousness. Milk is food that has been consumed by the eater then converted into an easily digestible form for another. It fills but cannot sustain like solid food.

Testimonies are *road maps* that pinpoint our destination. But, Holy Spirit wants to be our *tour guide*, leading us on *our path* to fulfillment (Proverbs 16:9). Sermons and testimonies give us hope in tough seasons, so we don't take for granted gathering with those who would encourage us. But, His intent is for us to keep *our hearts joined to Christ.*

Have you ever heard a message from someone's mouth, and it was like God was speaking to your heart? That message, that divinely connected word, is just a taste of the entree He wants you to have.

He has given us access to His throne room; those heavenly places which far exceed another man's revelation. He wants us to know something so deeply, it can't be choked out by circumstance, pressure, and persecution; so convinced by it, it would be harder to deny the color of our own skin! What He means for us to have can't be watered down or stolen because it comes from Heaven, and once we *taste and experience Him* for ourselves, there's no going back!

Let's not be satisfied any longer with mere knowledge. Let's "taste and see that the Lord is good" (Psalms 34:8a ESV)!

GRAB YOUR JOURNAL!

What is God showing you at this moment?

In light of this revelation, how does this shift your thoughts and actions?

Check Your Heart

READ

Romans 14:1-4,

Romans 14:10-13,

1 Samuel 26:9,

1 Corinthians 1:27,

1 Corinthians 5:12-13,

Matthew 13:24-30

When the co-founder of the Trinity Broadcasting Network, the largest Christian network, passed away, the articles on the internet ran the gamut of sorrow to ridicule. Other than dressing rather flamboyantly and wearing too much makeup for my taste, I didn't know much about her. I'd never really watched TBN much, so I don't know her background or denomination. But, what really shocked me was the number of Christians who attacked. Whether they had valid points or a religious spirit, I don't know, but until I've done what she and her family have done to reach nations and give outlets to other ministries, my "valuable" opinion doesn't amount to much!

Each of us has areas of strengths and weaknesses, and in them, we still love and worship God. Whatever we do, we do as unto our Lord as trusted ambassadors to the world. Ultimately, we are accountable to Him alone. What He calls *one* to do may offend *our* mind, but in it, He *reveals our heart.*

For several years after God removed King Saul's anointing because of arrogance and disobedience, Saul sought to kill the young shepherd God intended to take his place. Twice, David could have killed Saul, but rather said, "Do not destroy him; for who can raise his hand against the Lord's anointed and be guiltless?" (1 Samuel 26:9 AMPC)

In Romans 14, we're told not to criticize other believers. Not that we shouldn't correct sinful attitudes or that leadership shouldn't protect the church from false doctrines, but we need to take into account the hearts of young Christians who are still figuring out kingdom life. When they read our Facebook posts, hear our conversations, and watch our responses, they should see Christ.

1 Corinthians 5:12-13 says we are to judge those who work among us, never

at the cost of their identity in Christ, but always with the purpose of growth or restoration. However, it's not up to us to judge another man's servant (Romans 14:4). After all, God called the prophet Isaiah to walk around naked for three years as a sign to the people (Isaiah 20). How would *we* have judged *that!?*

God confounds the wise by working through things or people we may deem as foolish. Perhaps some have less to lose than those who covet reputation. If someone already knows they have nothing to lose, they may give their lives more easily for the "something greater."

We, not the buildings, are the church; stones set in place by the Chief Cornerstone. Let's not be distracted from building His kingdom by poking holes in the walls. Let every word we utter be with humility of heart, with love and restoration at the forefront. Let's keep our focus on Holy Spirit and our disapproval submitted to Him. God knows how to speak to His servants and how to separate the wheat from the tares.

GRAB YOUR JOURNAL!

What is God showing you at this moment?

In light of this revelation, how does this shift your thoughts and actions?

Vain Thought, Vain Talk

READ

Psalms 141:3-5,

2 Corinthians 10:3-6,

Exodus 20:7,

Psalms 19:14,

Hebrews 11:6,

Philippians 4:6-9,

Leviticus 19:12,

James 3:11,

James 1:26,

Romans 12:1-2

I have always been a poor arguer. I could never think of those "snappy comebacks" in the heat of the moment. So, I'd walk away defeated, rehearsing what had just been said in my mind, only *then* to think of the best retaliation ever.

The mental tongue-lashing I gave was brutal and rolled around in my mind for hours or days. Yep! *That's what I would have said...if I would have thought of it.* Only by then, it was too late. How much time and energy had I given to futile, senseless thoughts? How much time was spent trying to correct injustice and justify myself in my imagination? My thoughts were in *vain*.

The Google Dictionary definition of vain is: Producing no result. In Ecclesiastes 1 and 2, Solomon concluded that much of the toil of life was nothing more than vanity. He talks of the futility of what is gained through reasoning and effort.

We are told in Exodus 20:7 not to take God's name in vain, and we have boiled this down to mean not using Him as a curse word. But, when we read it as defined it says, "Don't attach God's name without intention of a result." God's name is not to be associated with futility or fruitlessness, so when we say it, we attach it to faith.

The words and meditation of our hearts are to be pleasing to God. Without faith, we can't please Him, so our thoughts and words must be aimed like an arrow, or we miss the mark. To entertain futile and senseless thoughts is vain imagination and produces no good result. We will either become haughty and prideful or invested in our own victimization.

Either way, when we don't cast these thoughts down at the feet of Christ, we place them on the throne of our hearts. Satan knows if he influences our thoughts, he rules the outcomes.

This is why God is so adamant about renewing our minds and submitting our thoughts to His Word. He has ordained us to produce and multiply, bringing glory to His Name, representing Jesus through our lives. It is our top priority and greatest mission.

Neither self-defeating nor high-minded thoughts produce anything good. Let's keep watch over our tongues, guard our hearts, and get in agreement with God's Word all while aligning our thoughts with His thoughts toward us! He's a good Father, and we are passionately loved by Him!

GRAB YOUR JOURNAL!

What is God showing you at this moment?

In light of this revelation, how does this shift your thoughts and actions?

Living Memorials

READ

Philippians 3,

Deuteronomy 8,

1 Peter 2:4-6,

Luke 22:17-20,

Romans 8:38-39,

2 Corinthians 3:2-5,

Acts 9

Memorial Day, for many of us, is a time to honor the fallen by enjoying the freedoms so many of our military men and women fought and died for, whether by going to the military museum, a church Memorial Day service, a backyard barbeque, or a day at the beach, our hearts are full of gratitude. Since the birth of our country, the struggle to attain and maintain freedom has been celebrated with the thankful hearts of a nation.

How easy would it be to let our children simply enjoy the freedom we share, never understanding where it came from? And how ignorant would we be to live as if we had been defeated and under another country's rule while our flag waves our freedom? The decision of everyone in the armed forces to sacrifice their lives for a greater cause has had a lasting impact on the way we think and live.

In the Bible, we find God telling men to set up times, days, or places of memorials. Moses built twelve standing stones at the foot of Mount Sinai after receiving the Ten Commandments and other ordinances (Exodus 24:2-4). The Israelites erected stone pillars to remember their miraculous crossing of the Jordan River (Joshua 4:2-3, 8-9). We continue to take communion as a memorial for what Jesus purchased on the cross for us (Luke 22:17-20). They are testimonies of God's deliverance or greatness.

Once we have made Christ *Lord* of our lives, the things of the past must lose their hold or they are still lording over us. Philippians 3:13 tells us to forget those things that are behind us and press forward, but in the verses prior to it, Paul tells us how he used to persecute the church before Christ. What he didn't do is waste time wallowing in regret, allowing his past to keep him from His calling. The marker for his change was the day he met Jesus on the road to

Damascus (Acts 9).

There are gifts and callings God has placed in our lives, and we are to be living letters read by those who see us, testifying of the Anointed One in our lives. To continue to try and breathe life into a dead past, as if we were practicing humility, not only wastes time but steals honor from the God who delivered us from it. Our testimony is that we were once *very* lost, and now we are *very* found.

Let's remember what the cross of Christ *purchased for us*. Let the place where He was made a curse for us, be the memorial for our freedom! Let's take communion often in our prayer time to discern the righteousness we've been clothed in and the healing He provided. His life, death, and resurrection is the marker of our freedom, and how we represent Christ just may be the marker for someone else.

GRAB YOUR JOURNAL!

What is God showing you at this moment?

In light of this revelation, how does this shift your thoughts and actions?

A Bad Sensor

READ

Genesis 1:26-30,

2 Corinthians 5:14-21,

Romans 3:22,

Colossians 1:12-14,

Romans 8:10-12,

John 3:1-7

A warning light came on in my car. My family calls it the "idiot light." It's the little "check engine" light people ignore as long as the car is running fine. Another light came on several months ago, telling me my tire was low. However, I knew the tires were fine, as I recently had them checked. A code reader also proved the engine was just fine. The problem turned out to be a bad sensor. It needed to be replaced before my entire dashboard lit up like a Christmas tree.

My sensor was telling me there was something wrong with something which was right. It had me thinking my engine needed extensive work, all because it was seeing things through a damaged connection. If I left the sensor broken, I'd have to rely on my ability (or lack thereof) to sense how my vehicle feels or sounds while I'm driving. Does it shimmy? Sputter? Skip?

This is what it's like when our minds are not renewed to Christ (the anointing) after we are born again. God has taken us out of the kingdom of darkness and placed us into the kingdom of light. He has taken we who were dead and made us alive. We are *new creations*! If we persist in associating our identity with what we've done and who we've been, rather than who we are in Christ, we have a bad sensor, and we will continue to *pay* for something that has already been repaired *through* Christ. To hold onto regret or excuse our old attitudes by saying, "This is just how I am," tells God *His sacrifice* wasn't *enough* for us.

One of my favorite motivational speakers, Andy Andrews said, "Successful people make decisions quickly and change their minds slowly. Failures make their decisions slowly and change their minds quickly." Salvation is *instant*, but learning to *walk in it* is a lifelong process. It takes *time* to change our world view to Christ's view. It takes *effort* to see a stumbling block as a stepping stone. It takes *determination* to get back up and brush ourselves off if we fall. It takes *humility* to repent when we've wronged someone. *Beating ourselves up is a fruitless waste of time.*

When we were born again, we were made completely righteous in God's eyes because He HONORS *the blood payment.* For Him to reject us would be to dishonor Jesus' sacrifice. So, why do we continue to allow our past to condemn our future? Why continue to see as wrong what has been made right?

If we are having trouble forgiving ourselves, let's start by meditating on what was purchased for us by honoring the blood payment, then we can fix our sensor by fixing our heart on God and what He says about us! When our thinking changes, it affects our choices, which affects our habits, which affects our lives, which affects those in our circle of influence, and their thinking, choices, habits... You get the picture.

GRAB YOUR JOURNAL!

What is God showing you at this moment?

In light of this revelation, how does this shift your thoughts and actions?

Unity

READ

Luke 6:32-36,

Luke 15:1-10,

John 15:18-20,

John 13:34-35,

Ephesians 4

My pastor, Al Brice, of Covenant Love Church in Fayetteville, NC, said when he started our church, he prayed God would give him a church that looked like Heaven, with diverse cultures, colors, and revelation, and there is so much *life* there because of it! God has called us into unity of the faith, with our hearts knit together, not our personalities and callings and maturity levels. We learn and *expand* our hearts and thinking through love in unity with diversity and *sprinkled* into society to manifest Christ.

There is a huge misunderstanding about unity. The world's idea of unity is when we all think and act as *one*. That isn't unity. It's *conformity*.

The world only knows how to love those who have the same mind. They can only find peace in compliance. They disdain anything which convicts them of their sin and will do whatever they can to belittle the Christian into coming off their "holier than thou" attitudes. They see anyone who lives according to God's Word as a threat to their way of living. We have been given the divine ability to love those whose values and ideologies are in direct opposition to God because Christ lives in us.

For us, their hatred and railings against the things of God shouldn't cause offense, but rather, let it be an invitation to pray for God to bring revelation. In some ways, it's easier to pray for them because their attitudes are manifested. It's harder to see when someone secretly holds those attitudes in their heart.

Unity is like harmony in music. It requires different parts working together on one page. Unity is different bodies, gifts, mentalities, and hearts who have at least one thing in common. Jesus was able to take twelve men with differing backgrounds, personalities, and flaws, and bring them together to change the world.

For Christians, the common ground is God's love patterned in the life of Jesus Christ. We all come from different backgrounds, nationalities, customs, races, politics, etc., but our unifying goal is to reveal the Kingdom of God to Earth.

Jesus called us to be *in* the world, not *of* it. We are on assignment from Heaven, all having different orders and instructions, so we learn to live in *this* world while we walk in *another*. We are sprinkled into the world system as a leavening agent, changing the atmosphere wherever we go. We love the ungodly as Christ does. Our love for them should confuse and convict, while tearing away the blinders the Devil has placed over their eyes.

We *cannot* have unity without diversity. We serve one God, and He has commanded us to love one another as Christ loved the church. The world will know us by our love for one another (John 13:34-35)! Let's enjoy and appreciate the *diversity which brings harmony*. Life would be boring without it!

GRAB YOUR JOURNAL!

What is God showing you at this moment?

In light of this revelation, how does this shift your thoughts and actions?

Time to Grow Up!

READ

James 4:1-17,

1 Corinthians 13:1-13,

Colossians 2:6-7,

Hebrews 6:1-2,

James 1:2-4,

Romans 5:3-4,

Colossians 3:16,

Hebrews 9:14,

Luke 14:25-27,

Proverbs 16:7

A toddler throws a temper tantrum in the grocery store. We've seen or been a part of that story. He wanted something and he was being denied. If the outburst works, the parent gives in, either from indulgence, exhaustion, or embarrassment, and the child learns *his behavior determines the outcome*. If not corrected, he will continue to use an emotional response to manipulate his parents. It's not that he doesn't love his parents, but his desire takes over, and he's too young to navigate being denied or delayed. As he becomes an adult, he may not realize his behavior was formed during that time, but now he will use emotions to manipulate his way through life, having learned to live by his senses.

We've been raised in a sin-dominated kingdom. In essence, we were homeschooled in the wrong home. There are people who have love for God but also see Him as a benevolent benefactor who allows them to remain willful under the guise of grace. They have not been renewed to a kingdom lifestyle. Jesus said in Luke 14:27 (TPT), "... anyone who comes to me must be willing to share my cross and experience it as his own, or he cannot be considered to be my disciple."

We all have areas of life we haven't fully submitted to God's authority, whether it be gluttony, politics, self-promotion, laziness, sexuality, offense toward someone that keeps us from loving well or any number of other things we are either not fully aware of or *choose* not to submit. We believe our rights and opinions to certain ideologies excuse ungodly behavior as being under grace.

If someone challenges our beliefs, we may see them as legalistic and become offended (James 4:1). We throw up a wall to protect our beliefs or behaviors, effectively cutting off either the person or a revelation. We forget that when opposition comes, it's to either *knock us off* God's Word *or* to *reveal a truth* we've yet to see.

My mom once gave me some advice for unsolicited input, "Chew up the meat and spit out the bones." There could be a seed of truth in that, even if the delivery was wrong. Don't run from *truth*, but examine the source, what's being said, and how we're receiving it. But, do so without going into self-condemnation. Judge the word without judging the person who saw something in us, even though *they* may have misread what they saw. They may have either misread a situation or have filters that keep them from seeing properly. If our desire is to mature, we should at least look at what we might be *projecting* to the world.

We pray. We seek God. We seek His wisdom that *always* lines us up with His Word. We purify our hearts by yielding to truth while *dismissing any lie that tries to sneak in with it.*

We do this by *knowing* we are not our own. We are loved by a Good Father who gave *everything* for a relationship with us and who tears down anything that gets in the way of His love manifesting and our growing up in Him.

Let's not live by the fear of letting go of old behaviors and beliefs which are dead works. Let's put away our worldly way of handling or manipulating people and situations and grow up into God allowing others to see Holy Spirit at work in us and bring glory to our Father!

GRAB YOUR JOURNAL! | *What is God showing you at this moment?*

In light of this revelation, how does this shift your thoughts and actions?

Distracted

READ

Hebrews 12:1-2,

Psalms 23:5,

Mark 4:13-20,

Genesis 1:28,

James 4:8,

2 Timothy 3:10-17,

1 Corinthians 2:12-16,

Romans 12:1-2

I admit; I'm easily distracted. I can walk into a room and forget why I went there. If the TV is on, I have to pause it for an extended conversation. I can even get distracted mid-sentence. I keep saying to myself, *Am I a little attention deficit and was never diagnosed, or is this just part of my personality?* I started praying and found myself, once again, distracted by my surroundings; the pile of clothes left unfolded, the plans for the day, the urge to check social media. When I snapped back to my intention, I asked God to help me focus, and He showed me a mental parable.

I saw myself in full armor, running alongside my battle buddies toward the enemy coming up the hill. As we shouted our battle cry in one voice, I could see the tops of the heads of our enemies and the dust behind them as they crested the hill. When they came into full view, there was one headed straight at me, holding out a golden labrador puppy. As the battle clashed around me and the dust surrounded us, all I was aware of was the puppy. I was taken away from battle by a simple distraction (Hebrews 12:2). God was showing me patterns of thought which He aimed to correct.

Psalms 23:5 says God prepares a table before me in the presence of my enemies. I believe, not only does He want us to eat of His goodness, but He desires we would be focused on only Him, while the enemy rages around us. Imagine the Devil's indignation watching us party at God's table, unmoved by the impending attack. How difficult would it be for us not to be a *little* distracted? Yet, God wants us to be *full* of this kind of unwavering faith.

Hebrews 12 says we are to fix our gaze on Jesus, and not be entangled with any hindrance which could easily trip us up. Mark 4 says the cares of life, the seduction of wealth, or desire for other things will choke out God's Word, producing no fruit in us, which is Satan's goal. He doesn't care if we are Christians, so long as we don't subdue and multiply (Genesis 1:28).

The Apostle Paul encouraged Timothy to hold *tightly* and continue in all he had been taught because things would happen which could draw him off track. If we're to hold tightly to Him, it's because we're going to experience things which will pull at us and cause us to lose our grip. God wants to fully invade our prayer life, binding us to Him so completely to make us unshakable, un-breakable, and un-distractible.

There are so many issues seeking our attention, but we can't go because we have an invitation to a feast with our God. His feast is meant to permeate fleeting thoughts. We should actually thank God our prayers are *so effective* that the Devil is *intimidated* into throwing darts of distraction. He fears how dangerous we are becoming to him as we enter into the secret place of the Most High (Psalms 91)!

GRAB YOUR JOURNAL!

What is God showing you at this moment?

In light of this revelation, how does this shift your thoughts and actions?

Don't Sit in the Ashes

READ

Colossians 1,

2 Corinthians 5:17,

John 3:1-8,

Colossians 3:1-10,

Romans 8:1-10,

John 15:12-15

If I was in a burning building, close to perishing by flame, and you came to rescue me, I would not ask for your credentials as a firefighter in order to follow you. I wouldn't care about the sins of your past or if you made terrible life choices. Or, what if you were trained in fire and rescue, and broke through to where I was trapped, then made excuses why you were unworthy to save me, leaving me there to die?

Yet, this is often what happens to Christians when we come into the kingdom of God. We allow the shame of *what we were* to frame *who we are* and *where we're assigned*, even though God's Word tells us we are a *new creation*; one which never existed before. We are *born again*!

Colossians 3:3 says we are dead, and our life is hidden with Christ in God. So, to carry our past around with us would be like dragging a corpse! Rather than becoming paralyzed by where we came from, we should honor His blood by receiving new life.

We've all made life-altering mistakes. We may have to live with the consequences of our sin. But, we can still be free from the guilt that binds us to it. Moses, David, and Paul were all murderers, yet they wrote much of the Bible under the influence of God-breathed words. They did not allow the consequence of their past to undermine God's plan for their lives.

There's not room for two on the throne of our hearts. It's either Jesus as Lord or our dead past. Let's not allow our old nature to be Lord of our lives. Romans 8 says thinking like a natural man will kill us! There is *no* condemnation when we *follow* after Holy Spirit!

We made the choice to *leave* a life that wasn't working for us in the first place. We fully understand we were *lost*! Our lives are not about who we were, what we did, or what was done to us which made us feel a certain way! We are delivered from those things, and they should only be used as our testimony to free others who may be trapped in the same burning buildings we were rescued from!

Our lives are about the *One who loves us*, not the past we escaped from! Let's allow our *deliverance* to be a road map to freedom for others and honor the blood of Jesus by walking in our destiny instead of sitting in the ashes.

GRAB YOUR JOURNAL!

What is God showing you at this moment?

In light of this revelation, how does this shift your thoughts and actions?

What's Your Motivation?

READ

1 John 4:7-21,

John 15:13-17,

John 4:6,

John 4:31-38,

Romans 12:1-2,

Matthew 16:24-26,

Hebrews 12:1,

Isaiah 40:28-31,

James 4:6,

Mark 12:30-31

What motivates you in your walk with Christ? What fuels your commitment to how you serve in the church? In how you treat your family, co-workers, and friends? What internal value makes you get out of bed every morning? If our answers to any one of those questions are not centered on love, then we will find ourselves tired, offended, burned out, frustrated, and overworked. Let me preface by saying we need time away to restore our natural body. Even Jesus needed rest.

When I say, "centered on love," I'm talking about *becoming selfless love*. Anything less is functioning outside of our created purpose. If our motivation is self-satisfaction, a need for acceptance, justification, or promotion, our hearts will be divided, and we will fall short of *empowering* grace.

We could speak eloquently, prophesy, have deep revelation, and mountain-moving faith, but if our actions don't match our words, we're nothing but noise (1 Corinthians 13:2). 1 John 4:20 tells us we're phonies if we say we love God and hate a brother. Verse 8 of the same chapter says if we don't love people, then we *don't really know* God. Our attitude for others who may not love us back is birthed from a heart which is grateful to God who loved us before we *ever* cared about Him.

We are not born again just to have the right to pray for God to fix our lives, to receive blessings, to attain some kind of justification for our condition. If our goal is simply to get to Heaven, we will live a miserably defeated existence, striving and fighting to have our own way. We are not born again just to go to Heaven. We are born again to *get Heaven inside of us. This* is our motivation.

There are so many things which may be broken in our lives, but do we come to Jesus because we want Him to fix us just so we can continue to function in our messes? His plan is not simply to *put a bandage on a wound* but to *restore us through transforming and renewing our thinking*. When our motivation changes, our decisions begin to change. When decisions change, our direction changes. When our *entire* motivation is to *become like Jesus*, circumstances which once held us captive are powerless. Suddenly, we're not obligatory, stressed out, or manipulative, trying to make life easier for ourselves. We are able to pick up the cross and run through every injustice, every unfairness, secure in *ever increasing love*.

We were created *by* Love, *for* love. Let's pursue the revelation of how much our Heavenly Father loves us and everyone around us. Mark 12:30-31 (AMP, emphasis added) says, "And you shall love the Lord your God with *all* your heart, and with *all* your soul (life), and with *all* your mind (thought, understanding), and with *all* your strength… You shall [*unselfishly*] love your neighbor as yourself. There is *no other* commandment greater than these."

Let's make our motivation to have this God-kind of love for others. Let's rethink our priorities, cutting away those things weighing us down, things working against His grace. We might be surprised we can actually soar with renewed strength as eagles, can run and not be weary, and walk and not grow faint.

GRAB YOUR JOURNAL! | *What is God showing you at this moment?*

In light of this revelation, how does this shift your thoughts and actions?

Compassion Without Compromise

READ

James 1:26-27,

Galatians 5:13-26,

Ephesians 4:1-21,

Proverbs 14:12,

1 Corinthians 13:1-13,

1 Corinthians 3:6-7,

Isaiah 61:3,

Matthew 6:33,

John 15:8

To me, it seems as if the world's idea of compassion is giving people a nice little wagon to carry the weight of the boulders of sin they've been dragging around. They make it socially acceptable, or ignore the burden, so they are seen as open-minded. But, God's idea of compassion is actually removing the boulders. Since the world doesn't have hope, there is nothing on which to attach faith. Those who are deceived simply don't know the power of being born again into Christ. So when, as Christians, we speak of releasing or removing the weights of twisted identities in people, we are seen as either arrogant or hateful.

Compassion and empathy are often misinterpreted. We are not to allow the sin which rules and reigns in society to become our normal. While we are not to be hateful, condemning or judgmental, we are still to stay unspotted from the world (James 1:27). Our lives shouldn't bend to what society deems normal at the expense of what our anointed Christ paid to redeem us from on the cross.

Ephesians 5:6 (TPT, emphasis added) says not to *"be fooled by those who speak their empty words and deceptive teachings."* Proverbs says, "You can rationalize it all you want and justify the path of error you have chosen, but you'll find out in the end that you took the road to destruction" (Proverbs 14:12 TPT).

We tend to veer off the path in either one direction or the other. We have to be careful about the little thoughts and attitudes which can slip through, in the name of compassion, taking us off track. We might have the tendency to bow to the media gods, basing our opinions on the flavor of the day depicted on social media, talk shows, the news, or from politicians. We set ourselves against God by giving *those things* priority over *His Word*.

Or, we may drive off the other side of the road, throwing up our religious front, whether in frustration or defensiveness, becoming loud clanging cymbals with no expression of Love. This is the *very behavior* Jesus rebuked over and over again in the lives of the Pharisees.

The deceptions overtaking lives are *never* going to be made right by our agreement. But, *neither* are they going to be won by our anger and protests. When we turn our eyes and hearts toward Christ, humble ourselves under His hand, and listen to Him, the supernatural power of Love will begin to work through us. We must live above what the world believes about the church, letting our lives prophesy the love letter from Heaven; the example of humility, deliverance, and salvation in *every* area.

Let's place the value of the cross on one another, practicing compassion, empathy, and unselfishly seeking God's best, just as Christ loved the church and gave Himself up for us. Let's start *influencing* those God puts in our lives by being fruitful trees of righteousness the world can eat from! Plant seeds of compassionate love and let Holy Spirit bring the increase!

GRAB YOUR JOURNAL!

What is God showing you at this moment?

In light of this revelation, how does this shift your thoughts and actions?

Free from Guilt and Shame!

READ

Psalms 27:1-6,

Hebrews 12:11-15,

Romans 12:18,

Hebrews 10:19-25,

1 John 2:16 (Amp),

2 Corinthians 5:17,

Ephesians 2:1-10,

Philippians 4:6-8,

Zechariah 9:12,

James 4:5-10

Driving down the road one day, a thought popped into my head about some shameful behavior I did as a teen. It made me physically wince, and I shivered to shake it off. *How stupid of me!* I thought. *After all, it's not who I am! I would never act that way now.* For me to avoid a person or a place to this day because of a constant reminder of my own embarrassment would be foolish. That memory was an attack, meant to lock me in a self-made prison to see myself according to the act, rather than who I am now.

If we have personally wronged someone, we should try to make amends or ask forgiveness, even if our attempt is refused. We have the ability *in Christ* to continue to pray and love, or, if we must, walk away, with a clean conscience and the ability to pray for the one we've wronged.

The truth is, shame is actually a form of pride. We may feel, since we are responsible for the act, it's our responsibility to carry it. To lay it down would seem as if we weren't sorry. Instead of humbling ourselves in repentance, we end up becoming the jail keepers of our own prisons.

Guilt, shame, and avoidance are tools of the enemy to keep us isolated and fearful, which can produce deadly results. When Adam sinned, he hid from God. When Judas denied Christ, his shame caused him to take his own life. Jesus told Peter that Satan's desire was to sift (or separate) the disciples like grain from the stalk, and that is *still* his mission. If the Devil can sift us from the place God has positioned us, he can reduce our effectiveness and better attack God's plans for our lives.

I've heard it said, "Jesus didn't come to make bad people good. He came to make dead people alive." We cannot live in fear of our past. In God's eyes it does not exist, but we do. However, it doesn't belong to us. And, if we must visit it, we must do so through the filter of the blood of Jesus Christ, so we can see it as the lie that it was and who we now are in Christ: a *new creation* (2 Corinthians 5:17).

Any thought which causes us to feel fear, guilt, or shame is under the influence of a lie. If we sense fear, we should question its influence on our lives based on God's Word. God doesn't intend for us to live in fear of anything! He wants us to be established in Him and part of His Body! Prisoners of hope!

There's only room for one *ruler* on the throne of our hearts. Guilt and shame shouldn't even be in the room. Let's stop running from our past whether it be five seconds or fifty years ago. Let's humble ourselves in the sight of the Lord and let Him alone define who we are.

GRAB YOUR JOURNAL!

What is God showing you at this moment?

In light of this revelation, how does this shift your thoughts and actions?

Defend, Debate, or Denounce?

READ
John 8,
John 3:17,
Ephesians 2:4-10,
Romans 6:1-2, 2
Corinthians 12:9-10,
Galatians 2:19-21,
Proverbs 9:7-12,
Proverbs 1:5-7

Every parent or teacher has been asked, "Whyyyyyyy?" in a whiny, argumentative way. It absolutely grates the parental nerves, and the typical answer is, "Because I said so." Hopefully, this ends the matter, but occasionally, it's accompanied by a groan of rebellion, even if what was asked is followed. At times, I would try to give a *reason* why, because I *hated* to hear "because I said so" as a child. I thought it would encourage a helpful attitude. Instead, it gave them ammunition for their argument. Sometimes we should practice the art of shutting up, and sometimes, we should look beyond the question and talk to the heart or answer the question we wish they *would* have asked.

There were many times Jesus didn't give an answer or simply waited. Usually, it was when the Pharisees were trying to accuse or discredit Him. In John 8, an adulterous woman was brought before Him as they sought to trap Him between law and grace. Before He ever answered, He stooped down and wrote on the ground for a while. When they pressed Him, he went for their hearts.

If he had answered, "Stone her," the crowds would have dismissed His teaching of grace. If he had released her, they would have denounced Him as a false prophet, against the law of Moses. He had to *reveal their heart* by letting them *feel the weight of their response.*

When God's Word is *obvious*, what is our response? Do we excuse ourselves because our rights have been violated? When we question God or people, we need to look at the intent of our hearts. Are we trying to justify selfish or sinful attitudes or actions? Are we looking for relief? Are we trying to make God's Word fit into our agenda?

After Jesus answered them, they dropped their stones and left. But, He still needed to address the woman in her sin. His grace didn't tell her, "Hey, you're okay like you are. You've been hurt so you deserve a little happiness." But, He also didn't go for her jugular and beat her with His words. Grace allowed her to understand she was *able* to "go and sin no more." His grace *empowered* her to go and make a better decision, knowing *forgiveness* saved her from certain death (Ephesians 2:4,10).

Grace which doesn't bring about change is deception. God's strength is greatest when we are at our weakest. In other words, when we quit deceiving ourselves into believing we know it all and we "got this" and place our confidence in Him, we open our hearts to hear from Heaven. His directives are meant to commission us. His promises are to strengthen us. It's our faith in His Word which shifts our hearts and minds. Our response is expressed in our obedience.

Before we ask our questions, let's examine our hearts. Are we determined to protect and *defend* our position? Are we looking to *debate* the issue to win an argument at the expense of ministry and relationship? Or, are we ready to *denounce* sinful attitudes and directions and humbly lay our arguments before Jesus Christ?

GRAB YOUR JOURNAL!

What is God showing you at this moment?

In light of this revelation, how does this shift your thoughts and actions?

Jesus Didn't Die Because I Was a Sinner

READ

Matthew 9:36,

John 3:16-17,

John 12:47-48,

James 3:16-18,

2 Corinthians 9:8,

Ephesians 3:20,

Psalms 23,

Hebrews 10,

John 17:1-26

When I heard the title of this devotion in a sermon, it shifted something in my spirit. Jesus gave His life, because we *sinned*, not because we are still *sinners*. I believe He died because we were lost children. If our identity is still *"sinner,"* we are simply *forgiven sinners* and our mindset will feed on our depravity. The "sinner saved by grace" attitude sounds like humility, but, in fact, keeps us *confident* in *our ability to sin*.

Jesus sacrificed Himself because we were God's children who had fallen into sin, and He came to *restore* us to life as it was before Adam ate from the tree (Luke 19:10).

God saw us like sheep without a shepherd (Matthew 9:36). His cross wasn't meant to judge us as how horrible and lost we were but to *remove* sin, *reveal* our value, and *restore* our purpose. His cross was about our identity as sons. If we woke up each day with a sin consciousness, we would be relying on our own ability to be worthy enough for His assistance, afraid to fail, and avoiding fellowship with Holy Spirit. And if we *happen* to *feel* like we've been good enough to gain His favor, then disaster strikes, we become offended, confused, and deceived into self-righteousness (James 3:16). Life and circumstance come to define us, and suddenly, we can become more focused on what we're going through than what we are becoming.

However, if we wake up knowing we are His beloved son or daughter, no matter what junk we walk through, we are confident in our Father, who abounds toward us all grace and sufficiency (2 Corinthians 9:8). Knowing who we are teaches us about our authority to bring Heaven to Earth. It's about His presence in us, manifesting Himself to the world, and bringing glory to Him! It's realizing our trials are not about *us*! Then we can go about our Father's business, restored to our purpose, potential, and destiny, staying in fellowship, learning how to navigate the hard places, fearing no evil *because He is with us* (Psalms 23:4)!

Let's shake off this sin consciousness which keeps us tied to second best (Hebrews 10:19-21). It's time to see ourselves as *God sees us*. His cross exposed our potential and value. He saw great value in what we could be if He lived inside of us, so let's become what He prayed and paid for in John 17; to be made Holy, fully equipped, and commissioned as His body! Let's love Him with *our* lives since He loved us with *His*!

GRAB YOUR JOURNAL!

What is God showing you at this moment?

In light of this revelation, how does this shift your thoughts and actions?

Are You Hangry?

READ

Romans 14:17,

Proverbs 3:5-8,

Galatians 5:13-26,

Deuteronomy 8:5-9,

Ephesians 5:18 (AMP),

John 4:13-15,

John 3:34,

Psalms 119:103,

Isaiah 58:11

My husband and daughter are alike—they both get angry when they are hungry. At first, they can't figure out what's wrong. Their sugar gets low, they become frustrated, can't think straight, and may even snap at someone when asked a question demanding thought. I figured this out early on, and instead of getting mad at them, I'll suggest they eat something. During our church's Daniel Fast, when sugar addictions are breaking, I've been known to duck behind the kitchen cabinet and hurl a bite-sized candy bar into the living room toward them like a grenade, shouting, "Incoming!" The point is, *I* can often detect the need before *they can.*

We can experience this in our spiritual lives also. We find ourselves in situations which appear easy enough, so we don't always consider the leading of God. Then, when it has gone sideways on us, we get anxious or frustrated, and our anxiety spills over into other areas of our lives. We walk heavier, slam doors, or tune out. Usually, those who are closest to us see it before we do, but if we're not careful, we'll offend *more* than a cabinet door.

We may wonder what's wrong, become self-focused, lose heart, and miss hearing Holy Spirit who is dwelling in us. When we finally make it back to church on Sunday, our pastor points us back to the banquet table. The grand question is, *Why do we often try out all our options before we finally come to the realization we need God in our situation?*

Proverbs 3:6 (KJV) says to "*acknowledge* Him" in all our ways. We interpret acknowledge as giving someone a *nod of recognition.* But, the Hebrew word is translated as *the kind of intimacy between a married couple to conceive.* It means to *know God* in a certain area of life. Whether we're struggling with an addiction, intercession, or problem, our prayer should be, "God let me *know* you in this area. Let us be as one in this and see myself and this issue as You do." Then, open yourself up to His direction, rather than keeping Him as your last option.

His Water, which will cause us to never thirst again (John 4:14), is the deep relationship with Holy Spirit, and He longs to fill us without measure. If we don't taste Him and see His goodness, our spiritual "sugar" will get low, and we won't see why things aren't quite right.

Let's be as intentional in our time with Holy Spirit (whether morning or evening) as we are on that first cup of coffee or our necessary food so we can go through our day, *energized* with the *fullness* of Him!

GRAB YOUR JOURNAL! | *What is God showing you at this moment?*
| *In light of this revelation, how does this shift your thoughts and actions?*

Fearing Man, or Fearing God?

READ

Mark 8:34,

John 15:18-27,

Matthew 5:14-16,

Philippians 2:1-16,

Isaiah 50:4-10 (AMP)

In my grandparents' day, people lived by the adage that your reputation is the only thing you really own. They guarded it, making sure the family name stayed of the utmost respect in the community. One didn't make any wave, rock any boat, or go against any grain which could stir controversy that "would just kill yo' mama" if she found out. There were things that "ladies just shouldn't do," and places no self-respecting person would go.

God has called many people to do things which appear culturally unsettling. He has called us to be different, to go crossways against the grain of the world. Some of the modern heroes of the faith surely had to cross some lines drawn by man to establish what God wanted to do in their era.

Fifty years after the Civil War, an African American pastor named William Seymour began the Azusa Street Revival in Los Angeles, stirring controversy by bringing the races together. His legacy has traced to the rise of nearly 600 million charismatic and Pentecostals worldwide.[6] Oral Roberts, during the height of segregation, refused to speak anywhere that the races were separated.[7] Polly and Smith Wigglesworth preached on street corners with the Salvation Army, joyfully enduring the scorn of some who would throw vegetables at them.[8] They were controversial then, but are now *heroes* of our faith!

As Christians, we are meant to be a light which shines brighter than the world around us. We cannot bow to the culture of the day, the criticisms of the blinded, or stay quietly in the corner because we fear what people will think if we step out in love and passion for Christ. That light may hurt the eyes of some of those living in darkness, and the Devil will see to it that attitudes are stirred up against us. They persecuted Jesus, and we are of Him. But, if we live in such a way that our presence convicts people toward righteousness, not preaching condemnation, we will draw them with the warmth of His light, and our lives will give glory to God.

I saw a quote by Bill Johnson, pastor of Bethel Church in Redding, CA that said, "If you don't live by the praise of men you won't die by their criticism.⁹" As representatives of Christ, we live submitted to God. In Mark 8:34, Jesus said if we want to go after Him, we must first deny ourselves, take up our cross, and follow Him. Taking up our cross means living like Him, conforming to His example, with full access to all the cross bought for us, sonship with God and an all-access pass to His throne!

This is not a time to live or pray passively. His body is beginning to arise. Let's begin by asking God to teach and position us for His moves; these shifts in the heavenlies that will affect the atmosphere on Earth. Let's solidify our hearts and set our faces like flint (Isaiah 50:7) toward the battle, fearing God and loving man, so that no insult can wound us and no fear can stop us!

GRAB YOUR JOURNAL!

What is God showing you at this moment?

In light of this revelation, how does this shift your thoughts and actions?

Intense Pruning

READ
John 15:1-17,
Colossians 3:12-15,
Matthew 5:23-24,
John 4:14,
Proverbs 27:6,
1 John 4:7-9,
Romans 13:8-14,
Romans 12:1-2,
I Thessalonians 5:11,
Ephesians 5:1-2,
Mark 11:25,
Psalms 34:17,
Isaiah 41:10,
Galatians 6:2

According to Greek mythology, the warrior Achilles was invincible in every part of his body except for his heel. When his mother dipped him in the magical river Styx as an infant, she held him by his heel such that the river water touched and blessed every inch of skin except the only place by which she held him. Ironically, he was killed in battle when he was shot in that spot with an arrow.

Much like Achilles, I had built up an identity of invincibility in one certain area of my life. But when I was pierced by someone I loved, I fell apart. Guilt, shame, and frustration all came crashing in. I was totally taken aback by my reaction because it was far from the Godly response I talk about wanting to have.

My inexcusable mistake had hurt someone I loved, and I felt horrible. Their anger felt like a weight around my neck as I fell at Jesus' feet and poured out my grief. I wanted comfort, and it came, oddly in the form of a loving rebuke. I finally understood how the good Shepherd's "rod and staff" mentioned in Psalms 23 could be a comfort. He reigned me back in, calmed my tears, and adjusted my heart with one revelation. I was so glad I had time alone afterward for God to start the pruning process. And, I know He will be faithful to complete it.

As I wept, Holy Spirit began speaking, "It's not about you. Stop your crying. It's self-deprecating and it's wrapped in a false pride," (kind of like that "in-your-face" best friend, with no filter, who shocks you to get your attention). Hearing that, I knew to shut up because He had something important to reveal. As I stopped going down the rabbit hole of pity, a sudden flow of scripture sprang up like a well, pouring over wounds, causing me to repent, revealing truth, and pruning me so growth could occur. His Words pulled spiritual weeds, pruned back pride, and healed the hurt. Within one hour, my heart was established in joy. Love poured out of my spirit. I was able to pray about the situation and worship God over my loved one.

I know there are still areas of our relationship which need restoration, but I can work at it from Heaven's perspective rather than through selfish need. I can own my mistake, repent, and humble myself with a sincere heart, understanding that though I have hurt someone unintentionally, I can come at this without self-serving pride, living at the mercy of my own emotional abuse. I can hurt for the other person's heart and pray God brings peace to them. I can work on reconciliation without owing them anything but love. I can love freely without fear. While I know there is some heavy duty work to do, I know God is concerned about the condition of my heart, that I am able to see through His eyes and build up others, *representing* Him in all I do and wherever I go.

GRAB YOUR JOURNAL!

What is God showing you at this moment?

In light of this revelation, how does this shift your thoughts and actions?

Don't Become What You're Going Through

READ

Romans 12:1-2,

Mark 11:23-24,

1 Peter 2:9,

Romans 1:17,

Galatians 3:11,

Hebrews 10:38,

Philippians 4:11-12,

1 Timothy 6:12,

Ephesians 6:12,

Galatians 6:9,

1 John 3:18,

John 14:26

Life has an intrinsic way of shaping us by experiences. If someone is hurt by something at church, they can develop bitterness toward God. A child may have ill feelings because of a painful incident which can grow into bitterness toward a sibling or parent, and they harden their hearts. When someone is promoted over us, we might develop an ungodly attitude. You may have lost faith because you prayed for someone who didn't get healed. You could have been rejected because of your political or religious beliefs. As followers of Christ, we give up our rights to hold on to these things.

We preach the message of mountain-moving faith, but we don't always understand we are called to *live* by faith. We want the *power* to heal the sick, raise the dead, and cast out demons, which is great, but our *call* to live by faith outweighs getting a mountain to move.

It's great when mountains move, and we *should* go after that! But, if *who we are* is because of *what we can do*, our identity is wrapped up in power rather than sonship, and that's a misplaced and unstable identity. There's no way we will live strong or finish the race we're called to in that case.

If we are not *established* in Love, *seeking* God, and *renewing* our mind, then when things go wrong, we'll be distracted, overwhelmed, and become whatever we're going *through*. Our *situation* will become our identity, and we'll question His call on our lives.

How is it that the faith of God flowing through us to heal the sick is made powerless to change our attitudes and keep our hearts from offense? When we choose to hold onto our hurts and misunderstandings, we aren't fully operating in His love.

How can we stand on Philippians 4:13a (NKJV, emphasis added), "I can do all things through Christ," but leave out verse 11b, "I have learned in whatever state I am, to be content..."? God isn't merely concerned with what we go through, but how we go through. Are we white-knuckling our tough seasons, wondering where God is, or loving Him, confidently trusting in His love for us while we're in the middle of the fiery furnace?

We are in the world, not of it (John 17:16). God knew we'd have to fight the good fight of faith (1 Timothy 6:12), so He gave us weapons (Ephesians 6:11). He knew we'd wrestle with demonic forces (Ephesians 6:12), so He gave us authority (Luke 10:19). He knew we'd get tired (Galatians 6:9), so He gave us strength in joy (Psalms 28:7)! He knew we'd be uncomfortable, so He gave us a Comforter (John 14:26). He gave us Holy Spirit and His Word to always be with us. We are His dear children (1 John 3:18)!

Let's reexamine who or what has been sitting on the throne of our hearts. Are we representing Jesus, or, are we letting the world dictate and fashion us?

GRAB YOUR JOURNAL!

What is God showing you at this moment?

In light of this revelation, how does this shift your thoughts and actions?

Rescues Ain't Always Pretty

READ

John 15:18-25,

2 Corinthians 4:4,

1 Peter 4:12-19,

James 3:16-18,

1 Corinthians 8:1-3,

Acts 22:14-15,

1 Corinthians 3:5-7,

Luke 9:51-56,

Ephesians 2:8-9,

John 17:21

I was watching a YouTube video called, "Hope for Paws, Benji Rescue," and God showed me a parallel to what it's like sometimes when a soul is rescued. This lost little dog who had never experienced love, surviving on his own, was being rescued by an organization specializing in the rehabilitation of strays. They had cornered this scared, ferocious, matted ball of fur. When they first caught him, he flailed, growled, and bit the restraint. He had no understanding that these people were there to help change his life for the better. He had become *used to his condition* and *fear* kept him from being approachable. However, with tenderness, they were able to bring him in, bathe him, trim away the neglect, and place him with other pets who would teach him what it was like to be accepted as part of a family.

If you've ever tried to minister into someone's life who either didn't understand their need or became offended, you may have felt you'll never get through to them. Either they don't realize they need rescuing, or they've confused surviving in a lie with living in truth and abundance, becoming used to their lifestyle (James 3:16).

Whether you've been cursed at, ignored, marginalized, or had hostility aimed toward you, just remember, *you're in good company*! Jesus said those who hated Him would also hate us.

But, it's really not *us* they hate. 2 Corinthians 4:4 says that if the gospel is hidden, it's because the Devil has blinded them. We are to commit our souls to Christ for safe-keeping (1 Peter 4:19), guarding our hearts against offenses, never allowing what others *don't* see to influence what we do see.

Rescues aren't always easy or pretty, but we are not to become frustrated or offended when people reject the gospel, like Jesus' disciples did when they wanted to call fire down from Heaven when they were rejected (Luke 9:54). Jesus told us to *be* a witness, compared to simply witnessing. A witness is someone who *sees* and *hears*. We see and hear God. They don't understand what we have experienced through faith. Don't get me wrong; we are to study His Word and minister it, even in our imperfection, trusting the Author of our faith. But, unless we *become* what Holy Spirit is saying to us, we'll only be trusting our own knowledge, possibly trying to beat people into the Kingdom with it.

As those He has sent to change the world, we must remember we are to *represent* Jesus. It is we who plant and water, but only Holy Spirit brings the increase. Let's remain humble and not allow ourselves to become angry, pride-hurt, or frustrated, learning to trust our Father for what we've sown by His grace into the lives of a world that needs a Father.

GRAB YOUR JOURNAL!

What is God showing you at this moment?

In light of this revelation, how does this shift your thoughts and actions?

Heart vs. Law

READ

Psalms 138:2,

1 Corinthians 11:1,

Matthew 11:30,

Matthew 23:1-7,

James 4,

Micah 6:6-8,

Romans 8:1-17 (AMP)

When God gave Moses the Ten Commandments, people came up with over 600 extra laws to interpret what they thought God meant. The Pharisees of the day were in charge of studying and interpreting those laws. In order to maintain order and control, they believed they had the monopoly on how it should be carried out, but it was the unlearned people who bore the weight of it. It was in the name of keeping the Sabbath as a day of rest, the 'religious' mind was willing to free an animal from a pit, but condemned Jesus for freeing a crippled woman from her infirmity on the same day.

It seemed easier to follow a rule they could boast in keeping, rather than follow after God's heart. Those with access and ability to study the law, became the rulers and judges over people.

Religion without relationship seeps into Christianity when men choose to live by appearances alone. Rather than having an ear to hear God, some live by man-made religious rules, that were never in God's Word, making themselves appear holy. Their hearts are far from God, and the way they conduct their lives reflects God as a tyrannical slave driver, looking for a reason to strike humanity down.

It's easier to preach behavior modification, instead of teaching leaning into a relationship with Holy Spirit that will shape our foundation and give us truths to build on. We tell people to come to Jesus and allow Him to clean them up, but once they're born again, they're handed a "do this and be holy" list at the door. I'm all for teaching holiness, but it's the *transformed heart* that is *alive in Christ* that makes us dead to sin. We are to disciple by example (1 Corinthians 11:1).

Our lives should be a testimony of continually dying to self so Christ may live through us. It is the law of grace which empowers, putting to death the *self*-preserving, *self*-fulfilling, and *self*-righteousness. It is grace that allows our hearts to be ruled by love and our lives led by Holy Spirit.

We all have areas in our lives where we tried to make *God* fit, rather than submit ourselves to Him. Submitting to die to a desire or lifestyle seems impossible, but God never gives us a command His grace doesn't empower. Believing He esteems His Word, we rest in it, knowing He is the Author and Finisher. When we read, "Be not afraid," He's releasing the same authority when He created the world, saying, "Light *be*!" His words are *never* fruitless. He's *creating* faith and courage.

Let's trust in the amazing plan He has for us!

GRAB YOUR JOURNAL!

What is God showing you at this moment?

In light of this revelation, how does this shift your thoughts and actions?

Don't Lose Your Grip!

READ

John 6:35-69,

Hebrews 13:5-6,

John 10:27-29,

Hebrews 3:17,

Hebrews 3:19,

Mark 11:23,

2 Corinthians 4:13,

2 Corinthians 3:14-18
(TPT),

Hebrews 3:12 (AMP),

Jude 20-25,

James 1:5-8

The other night, I was playing with my daughter's goldendoodle. Holding the ends of a rope toy, I was almost able to pick him up as he grasped firmly with his teeth. But, after a few minutes of playing, he got distracted and relaxed his hold, and I was able to snatch it away.

This mini-wrestling match reminded me like my daughter's dog, we have to hang onto every truth we receive even more firmly because the Devil himself is going to try to wrestle it away. He will throw circumstances or "logical" thinking at us to get us to loosen our grip enough to snatch it away. That's why it's called the good "fight" of faith.

In John 6, beginning in verse 63, the crowds following Jesus become offended and reject Him because of what He is saying. Jesus turns to the twelve disciples and asks, "Are y'all gonna leave me too" (my southern Jesus translation)? Peter answered, "Lord, who else would we go to? *You alone* have the words of eternal life" (68). In other words, "*No matter what we don't understand*, somewhere in you are the answers, and our hearts burn with the desire to *know You more*."

In Hebrews 13:5b-6 (AMP, emphasis added), God says,
"'I WILL NEVER [under *any* circumstances] DESERT YOU [nor give you up nor leave you without support, nor will I in any degree leave you helpless], NOR WILL I FORSAKE *or* LET YOU DOWN *or* RELAX MY HOLD ON YOU [assuredly not]!' So we take comfort *and* are encouraged *and* confidently say, 'THE LORD IS MY HELPER [in time of need], I WILL NOT BE AFRAID. WHAT WILL MAN DO TO ME?'"

Let's not contaminate our faith with worry and fear because God is holding onto us as we navigate the trials and tribulations of life. Life doesn't always work out the way we planned. It doesn't always make sense. We must stop trying to *force things to work out*, trying to make God somehow fit our reasoning. We have this sense that we need to understand everything in order for us to have faith when the very *act* of faith surrounds an element of doubt. Applied, consistent faith is what causes doubtful situations to change!

Instability will cause us to receive nothing at all (James 1:5-8). We must *build ourselves up* in the most holy faith by praying in the Spirit and keeping ourselves in His love, expectantly looking forward to the mercy of our Lord (Jude 20-21).

GRAB YOUR JOURNAL!

What is God showing you at this moment?

In light of this revelation, how does this shift your thoughts and actions?

Renewing The Analytical Mind

READ
Philippians 3:4-11,
James 3:13-18,
1 John 3:2,
Ephesians 5:1-20,
Romans 8:28,
Jeremiah 17:5-8,
Luke 14:26-33,
Romans 12:1-2,
Hebrews 11:6

My husband is naturally an analytical thinker. He brings his analytic thinking into his born-again life, making faith a practical expression like a mechanic would use a tool. Analytical people have the ability to break down facts and thoughts into strengths and weaknesses. They're good at examining, recalling, and using information to solve problems. When my husband reads something in the Bible, he makes the adjustment in his heart, as if turning a bolt with a wrench. He used to wonder how people could wrestle with a truth when it is right there in black and white.

When analytical thinking is not born-again, it creates a chasm between logic and truth. It sees a person's actions and judges the external. It often defers hope when the worst seems inevitable. It questions or dismisses the Truth of God's Word against the presented facts and conventional wisdom. It will often establish itself in religious practices that require no faith rather than a relationship with Father God (John 5:39).

If we're reasoning to the point where we question Truth, we'll be deceived like Eve in the garden (Genesis 3:4). God gave us the ability to reason, but it was *never so we could talk ourselves out of Him*. When we submit our lives to Christ, we must humbly submit our reasoning to faith.

God saw us through the eye of truth to the point that, even while we were hostile, weak and imperfect, He sent His Son to die to reveal it to us. He is about *redeeming* life, not just rescuing the pitiful. So, we're not just to sing and pray to Him. We're to become *like Him*, following Him in demonstration and representation. When we *see* Him, we will be *like* Him. We must *allow* God to change *how* we see, turning our hearts to humility to say, "God, You know better than I things that have yet to be revealed, so I obediently submit my intellect, knowing that You love me and want the best for me." This is an act of faith in the presence of doubt.

How we feel will contradict Truth many times because we've been trained how to respond in a fallen world. The analytical mind, apart from God, will try to lessen the risk by holding something back to hedge itself against failure. If what we're thinking and believing doesn't encourage us and keep us moving forward, we have mixed in the wisdom of man, and it is no longer Truth. We cannot live righteously and divide our faith by placing part of it in our own strength. Faith is like a seed. An entire seed must be planted in Good Soil in order to grow. But, if that seed is split and planted in two different pots, it will produce nothing.

The born-again analytical mind will assess the risk but decides regardless of success or failure, pleasing God is far greater. He will ultimately work things out for the good of those who love Him. It's okay for us to count the cost, assess, and understand the risk (Luke 14:26-33), but if we make Jesus Christ *Lord* of our lives, it is our rational, intelligent act of worship (Romans 12:1) to make His Lordship the *pivot point* for all other decisions, *whether we can formulate the outcome or not.*

GRAB YOUR JOURNAL!

What is God showing you at this moment?

In light of this revelation, how does this shift your thoughts and actions?

The Right Tool for the Job

READ

John 14:25-27,

Jeremiah 29:12-13,

John 16:13-14,

Galatians 5,

James 1:5-8,

Proverbs 4:18,

Proverbs 27:17,

Jeremiah 17:5-10,

3 John 1:2,

1 Kings 3:9

We bought our home early in our marriage. I was so excited to be able to decorate and modify things the way I wanted them to be. Back then, I had no clue about power tools and not a lot of money to buy any, but I wanted a strip of chair railing down our hallway. Someone loaned me a little plastic box called a miter box which had grooves templated for angling a cut to go around corners. I placed the wood in it and cut it with a small hacksaw so the ends would meet at a proper 45 degrees. Even though I did a great job, a power miter saw would have allowed me to do the job in a tenth of the time and would have been much easier.

When we first come into the kingdom of God, we're a lot like that first-time home-buyer. We know how we want things to be, but we may be clueless about all the spiritual tools available to us. We watch other people, the church, seeing what they do and what they say. This isn't necessarily a bad thing. Iron sharpens iron (Proverbs 27:17). But, our primary goal should be learning from Holy Spirit. If we are building our lives around what we see others do, we will only be rooted in the shallow soil of the flesh. We mustn't simply copy the outward actions of Godly people. We must develop our ear toward Holy Spirit to build in us the everlasting foundation, rooted in His Kingdom, fully supplied.

If we are still trying to "work up" faith to move mountains because we've watched people pray a certain way, we may find ourselves falling short, or becoming discouraged at the lack of answers. We tend to look for methods when we are supposed to be listening to Holy Spirit.

God's primary focus is our relationship with Him. Even though miracles and doing good works are to play a part in our daily lives, God doesn't want our *identity* established in those things. In doing so, we're limited to good works but never exploring the places in His kingdom He wants to take us.

If having our prayers answered is just a way to get pressure off so we can continue the same path we were on before we were in trouble, we will hold God accountable for our lack or become guilt-ridden Christians always trying to gain God's favor.

Maybe, instead of asking, "Why isn't this working?" or "What is wrong with me?" which depletes us of power, accuses God, and validates our opinions, we should be praying and asking, "Where is it? How does this work? Give me wisdom. Show me, Holy Spirit! Mentor me in this area."

God desires us to prosper and be in health, *even as our soul prospers* (3 John 1:2). We can trust there is a power tool in His kingdom connected though a relationship with Him, which is better than any method we may be practicing just to get a result.

Instead of empowering the "why," let's focus on our relationship with Him, allowing Him to teach us. There is nothing "wrong" with us, other than the fact we are still growing up in Him. Let's be patient but stay hungry and open to hearing His voice, growing in the path of righteousness until we are as bright as the noonday sun!

GRAB YOUR JOURNAL! | *What is God showing you at this moment?*

In light of this revelation, how does this shift your thoughts and actions?

Praying for a
Loved One's Salvation

READ

Psalms 118:17,

Isaiah 54:13,

Romans 4:16,

Romans 4:21-24,

James 5:16,

Ephesians 1:17-23 (TPT),

Ephesians 3:17-21 (TPT),

Ephesians 5:8-17 (AMP),

Proverbs 4:23,

Ephesians 6:10-18,

Jeremiah 29:11-14,

Matthew 14:26-33

Have you ever prayed for someone close to you, a good friend or family member, who was spiritually lost? I have. And, in my experience, my heart's cry for their salvation as I watched them walk in paths leading to destruction overwhelmed my prayer life for far too much of it.

I poured out my heart, begged and pleaded, fighting all kinds of spiritual battles for a loved one for twelve years, and God has recently been showing me that it was only about the last two of those years that were effective for change. I found my prayers for them had become inundated with his hopeless state. They had been contaminated with frustration, anxiety, fear, and anger.

My mistake was focusing on how it was affecting me, rather than the deception my friend was bombarded with, forgetting to seek God's wisdom. I went through the Christian motions of praying but not really understanding how to *fight for him*. Even though I loved him, I was fearful he would get so far away from God he'd never find his way back, so I wrapped myself in a blanket of self-motivated prayer to alleviate the raging storm within me. Our relationship became strained, partly because sin had separated him but also because my desire for him to *get his life together* kept me from enjoying the *good parts* of him. I was so frustrated by his actions that my conversations were riddled with guilt and attempts at manipulation instead of ministering life.

Then one day, God changed my perspective. In the same way that God so loved the world that He gave His Son, sacrificially for me (John 3:16), not condemning me (John 3:17) and loving me while my heart was far from Him (Ephesians 5:8). He showed me how to intercede effectively, by using visible circumstances as pinpoints of prayer, so I prayed for his friends, open eyes, and a tender heart. I prayed for God to send laborers across his paths. I prayed for protection, declaring truths like Psalms 118:17 (AMP), "[He] will not die, but live, And declare the works and recount the illustrious acts of the Lord." I began to pray Paul's prayers for the church in Ephesians 1 and 3 until they became truth to me.

Once I decided to choose God's truth and promises over my own feelings, I was able to stand in the firestorm. My thoughts and words became intentional. I relinquished the desire to manipulate, and the fear he would die unsaved had to go. Instead of looking at what my loved one was *doing*, I chose to see him through God's eyes, see his created value to the point I was fully convinced in my heart that *God* would complete the work. I would not even allow myself to speak of his failings.

Don't get me wrong: the Devil kicked his attack into high-gear, and his behavior was increasingly worse before it got better. But, fully armed with Christ, I was now walking through the fire unscathed. I was still able to love and accept him and even *enjoy* his friendship. Yes, I still wept. Yes, my heart *suffered long*, but not because *I was offended*. *This* intercession was completely for *his* pain and deception. I refused to back off of it—no matter how long it took. I protected that seed of faith, entrusting only one other prayer partner who knew and prayed in agreement with me. No one else knew.

God began to show me in my trying to make Him fit into my own expectations, pulling back when it was uncomfortable and taking my eyes off of Him essentially tied His hands. It's only when I turned my instruments of war on the *real* enemy, that He could fight alongside me.

Let's begin to do battle *for* the lost; those twisted in deception. Instead of allowing ourselves to be pottered by what we see and feel, let's wield the sword of the spirit with precision. Let righteousness guard our hearts. Let the helmet of preservation keep our thoughts. Let us walk in peace, girded with Truth and shielded by faith so we'll be aware of all of Heaven's resources that have been made available! We're not fighting *against* people. We're fighting *for* them!

GRAB YOUR JOURNAL!

What is God showing you at this moment?

In light of this revelation, how does this shift your thoughts and actions?

Living By Faith

READ

Romans 1:17,

Galatians 3:11,

Hebrews 10:38,

Deuteronomy 31:6,

Hebrews 13:5-6,

Hebrews 4:11-16,

John 15:12-17 (AMP),

Acts 17:28-29,

1 John 4:10

Have you ever noticed the difference between a toddler and a more mature child when they need assurance by a parent in a scary or new situation? The toddler will cling tightly or look for the touch of the parent, but an older child may simply look to see their parent's eye is on them or if Dad is in the room to give them the courage they're looking for.

Our church holds an annual regional women's conference which takes an army of women to put together. It seemed no matter how tired most of us were by the end of it, the exuberance and expectation of manifestation carried us through a power-packed, God-kissed weekend! It was a time to get before our God and intimately lean into His presence.

But, what if you are the one who can't get that "conference experience?" There may be times we're sitting in a service, where obviously people are being touched by Holy Spirit. Yet, here we sit, wondering if and when this "feeling" is going to hit us. As we look around, we can begin to compare ourselves and wonder why we seem to be left out. We may think, *I'm not where I need to be in Christ, I yelled at the kids this morning and can't get into it*, or *God is holding out on me because...*" (Fill in the blank).

In judging ourselves, we empower those feelings, increasing the divide. We may believe we have to "get ourselves together" before He will allow us to experience Him, when actually, it is His love which draws us to begin with. Isn't it He who loved us before we loved Him (1 John 4:10)?

Could it be Father wants us to understand what it is to "live by faith?" Could it be He doesn't want us to be moved by what we feel or don't feel? If He holds back the goosebumps and tingles, maybe He is drawing us to a deeper understanding of love and faith; the kind that says, "I know You're in the room. *You dwell in me*, and *You love me*, and You will *never* leave me nor forsake me. So, I *worship You by faith*!"

There may be times we want to "experience" His touch, but if we become feelings-oriented, we'll begin to trust them instead of Him. Why would He do us the disservice of giving us a feeling to follow, when we are to be led by faith? Feelings are wonderful, but we are not to live by them. Could it be, like the older child, He wants us to know He is in the room, and He delights in us and is with us? If we seem to be carrying around empty buckets, shouldn't we worship as if we are holding that empty bucket up to Him, expecting to be filled?

Let's not shrink back because of our feelings or the lack of. Let's take Him at His Word that He will never leave us nor forsake us. We may find He is taking us to a new level of maturity in Him. He is bringing about a new confidence and boldness, not because we have a "feeling," but because we understand what He is saying.

GRAB YOUR JOURNAL!

What is God showing you at this moment?

In light of this revelation, how does this shift your thoughts and actions?

Awaken the Passion

READ

Ephesians 2:5-6,

John 20:22,

Genesis 2:7,

Luke 24:32,

John 10:2-4,

John 10:10,

Joel 3:9-17,

Isaiah 61:7,

Revelation 12:10,

Ephesians 6:13-18,

2 Corinthians 2:14,

Psalms 23,

Isaiah 58:8,

Romans 8:28-30,

Matthew 5:16,

Ephesians 3:14-20,

1 John 4:16-18,

1 Peter 1:7-8,

John 6:12

When my daughter finished her stint in the Marine Corps, she decided to go to school to be a physical therapy assistant. She has always wanted to do something with fitness or training but had no definitive direction. To apply, she had to complete shadowing hours at the hospital, where she enjoyed seeing different aspects of the job. One day, she came home overwhelmed with joy to the point of tears, saying, "I *know* that this is what I'm meant to do." Her *passion* had *found her*!

Many of her friends had already completed their educations, while hers was just beginning. She had felt like she was somehow behind, but now the winds of passion were in her sails to see her through. Her timing may not have fit the mold, but her calling had awakened at last. Everything she had been through had brought her to *this* point in time.

God never wastes anything (Romans 8:28). All we've been through gives us perspectives others may not have. He never remembers our sins, but He knows how to use our past for His glory and our victory. Jesus didn't come to make bad people good. He came to make dead people alive. He came to know us intimately and to be known *by* us, to reveal our identity and our purpose for living. He came to give us life abundantly (John 10:10).

He came to breathe into us (John 20:22), to ignite a fire that turns what caused us pain and shame into a force able to pull other lost children from the same torment (Joel 3:10). He came to equip us with an armor of righteousness and a shield of faith to extinguish the darts of the enemy that accuse us and take away life. He calls us to victory through the tribulations we've endured, so we can beat our enemy with the same life he tried to destroy. He longs for that "AHA!" moment where we see ourselves in our destiny to the extent that *nothing else* matters except partnering with Holy Spirit to build a lasting testimony that's bigger than we are. When our lives bring glory to Him, we are glorified (Romans 8:30).

That glory, to me, is the knowledge that my life is pleasing to my father God. Words seem to cheapen it to a feeling, but it's more of an inner confidence, a peace and quiet strength, joy, and contentment (1 Peter 1:7-8). I feel a light illuminating and overflowing in my heart causing my soul to praise Him, returning and giving all glory back to Him, even when I'm staring down burdens and trials (Ephesians 3:20).

Let's passionately seek to know God through Christ *above all else* and let Holy Spirit show us our heart's desire. Let Him breathe into our sails and awaken us to the passion and glory in knowing Him and our purpose.

GRAB YOUR JOURNAL!

What is God showing you at this moment?

In light of this revelation, how does this shift your thoughts and actions?

Acknowledgements

As a military family stationed at several places, it was my mom who would seek out our houses of worship. We visited many churches and denominations, and when we'd ask where we were going to attend, she would say, "Wherever the Holy Spirit is moving."

We have "eaten at many tables," and I believe there are things to be learned (whether God, good, or nice try) from all of them.

Most of my favorite ministers continue to add to the wealth of God in my life. From my pastors, Al and Tava Brice, from Covenant Love in Fayetteville, NC, to the constant stream of YouTube sermons by Dan Mohler, Todd White, Lisa Bevere, or Bill Johnson's crew from Bethel Church in Redding, CA, among others, they make me hungry for the "more" of God.

God has something to say, and if we'll just hush and listen, we'll hear Him in everything!

Notes

1) Johnson, Bill. "Reigning in Life." Facebook video, 00:25. January 30, 2018. https://www.facebook.com/ibetheltv/videos/10155979286730930/

2) "Polycarp's Martyrdom | Christian History Institute." Accessed May 22, 2020. https://christianhistoryinstitute.org/study/module/polycarp/

3) http://discerninghistory.com/2016/01/polycarp-the-man-the-flames-would-not-touch/

4) TV, Bethel. 2014. "You Have Authority | Bill Johnson | Bethel Church." YouTube. YouTube. June 2, 2014. https://www.youtube.com/watch?v=-tBok-Fra4Ks.

5) Andy Andrews: There Would Be No USA If... (LIFE Today / James Robison) https://www.youtube.com/watch?v=57I2EECFzTA

6) Pentecostal Movement Celebrates Humble Roots L.A.'s Azusa Street to Mark Centennial of Fast-Growing Religion Centered on Holy Spirit https://www.washingtonpost.com/archive/local/2006/04/15/pentecostal-movement-celebrates-humble-roots-span-classbankheadlas-azusa-street-to-mark-centennial-of-fast-growing-religion-centered-on-holy-spiritspan/99f69d68-e65e-44d4-87eb-6b192056d0e8/?noredirect=on&utm_term=.0e4a4bf447d5

7) Synan, Vinson. "Oral Roberts, Son of the Pentecostal Movement, Father of the Charismatic Movement by Dr. Vinson Synan, Noted Church Historian." Hugh's News. March 30, 2018. Accessed May 09, 2019. https://www.hughs-news.com/newsletter-posts/oral-roberts-son-of-the-pentecostal-movement-father-of-the-charismatic-movement-by-dr-vinson-synan-noted-church-historian.